LARSON, BOSWELL, KANOLD, STIFF

Passport
to Mathematics
BOOK 2

Alternative Assessment

by Cheryl A. Leech

Alternative Assessment includes information on using scoring rubrics, portfolios, error notebooks, math journals, and notebook quizzes. Also included are projects, mid-chapter partner quizzes, and individual and group assessments.

McDougal Littell
A HOUGHTON MIFFLIN COMPANY
Evanston, Illinois • Boston • Dallas

ISBN: 0-395-89650-9

3456789-PBO-02 01 00 99

CONTENTS

ASSESSMENT

The purpose of assessment in mathematics is to improve learning and teaching. It is imperative that assessment be used to broaden and inform, not restrict the educational process.

NCTM STANDARDS

With the advent of the standards for mathematics proposed by the National Council of Teachers of Mathematics (NCTM), the process of change in mathematics education has accelerated. No longer is the emphasis on computation. The emphasis is now shifting to include higher-order thinking skills, problem solving, and the ability to communicate mathematically. These new emphases do not so much require that a different type of mathematics be taught, rather that the mathematics be taught differently. These changes call for different types of assessment than the traditional paper-and-pencil tests and/or quizzes where there is only one answer and only the answer is evaluated. According to the *NCTM Curriculum and Evaluation Standards for School Mathematics,*

> *"Assessment must be more than testing; it must be a continuous, dynamic, and often informal process,"*
> (p. 203).

Alternative assessment is a means of evaluating student progress using several non-traditional assessment tools.

PURPOSE

According to the Mathematical Sciences Education Board (MSEB), there is a need for mathematics assessments that accomplish the following.

- Promote the development of mathematical power for all students.
- Measure the full range of mathematical knowledge, skills, and processes specified by the NCTM curriculum standards.
- Communicate to students, parents, and teachers what mathematics students already know, as well as the mathematics they have yet to learn.

WHO USES THE INFORMATION?

The information gathered by alternative assessment can be used in various ways. Students can use the information gathered through alternative assessment to appraise their own mathematical achievement and understanding. Teachers can use the information to make informed decisions about the instruction of their students. Administrators can use this information to evaluate the effectiveness of a mathematics program. And finally, policy makers would find this information invaluable for budget appropriations for mathematics education programs.

ADVANTAGES

There are several advantages to using a variety of measures of achievement.

- One type of assessment cannot serve all informational needs.
- Receiving information from multiple sources leads to more informed decision making.
- Traditional paper-and-pencil tests are incomplete measures of achievement.
- Using a variety of assessments is a more equitable measure of a student's mathematical progress. Many alternative forms of assessments have less potential for bias than traditional measures.

GOALS

The goals of alternative assessment are as follows.

- Find out what the student already knows.
- Evaluate the depth of the student's conceptual understanding, and his or her ability to transfer this understanding to new and different situations.
- Evaluate the student's ability to communicate mathematically his or her understanding, make mathematical connections, and to reason mathematically.
- Help plan the mathematics instruction necessary to achieve the objectives of the course.
- Report individual student progress and show growth towards mathematical maturity.
- Analyze the overall effectiveness of the mathematics instruction.

BIBLIOGRAPHY

Here are some additional sources of readings about alternative assessment.

Curriculum and Evaluation Standards for School Mathematics, National Council of Teachers of Mathematics, 1989.

How to Teach Math with USA Today, USA Today, 1991.

Mumme, Judy. *Portfolio Assessment in Mathematics*, California Mathematics Project, University of California, Santa Barbara, 1990.

Smith, Sanderson M. *Great Ideas for Teaching Math,* Portland, Maine: J. Weston Walch Publishing, 1990.

Stenmark, Jean Kerr. "Assessment Alternatives in Mathematics," *Equals*, 1989.

HOLISTIC SCORING

Some teachers hesitate to use alternative assessment methods because they are not sure of how to grade the assignments. One method that many educators have found useful is called holistic scoring. Mathematics educators have long used a similar method to evaluate a student's answer by first examining the answer and then analyzing the student's work if the answer is incorrect. Holistic scoring evaluates the solution as a whole, instead of focusing on only one aspect of the solution. To reach a final score, you must first identify aspects of the work that you consider necessary to the solution. Be sure to share your list with students. Here are some aspects of the student's work that you should consider.

- Understanding the Task
- How? Quality of Approaches or Procedures
- Why? Decisions Made Along the Way
- What? Outcomes of Activities
- Language of Mathematics
- Mathematical Representations
- Clarity of Presentation

Each of these aspects is discussed below.

UNDERSTANDING THE TASK

Sources of Evidence
a. Explanation of task
b. Reasonableness of approach
c. Correctness of response, inference of understanding

Final Rating
1. Totally misunderstood
2. Partially understood
3. Understood
4. Generalized, applied, extended

HOW? QUALITY OF APPROACHES OR PROCEDURES

Sources of Evidence
a. Demonstrations
b. Descriptions (oral or written)
c. Drafts, scratch work, and sketches

Final Rating
1. Inappropriate or unworkable approach or procedure
2. Appropriate approach or procedure some of the time
3. Workable approach or procedure
4. Efficient or sophisticated approach or procedure

WHY? DECISIONS MADE ALONG THE WAY

Sources of Evidence

a. Changes in approach

b. Explanations (oral or written)

c. Validation of final solution

Final Rating

1. No evidence of reasoned decisions

2. Some evidence of reasoned decisions

3. Reasoned decisions are used throughout

4. Reasoned decisions are explicitly discussed and adjustments are considered

WHAT? OUTCOMES OF ACTIVITIES

Sources of Evidence

a. Solutions

b. Observations and extensions (what if. . .)

c. Connections, applications, generalizations, syntheses

Final Rating

1. Solution without observations or extensions

2. Solution with observations or extensions

3. Solution with connections or applications

4. Solution with generalizations or syntheses

LANGUAGE OF MATHEMATICS

Sources of Evidence

a. Terminology

b. Notation and symbols

Final Rating

1. No use or inappropriate use of mathematical language

2. Appropriate use of mathematical language some of the time

3. Appropriate use of mathematical language most of the time

4. Use of rich, precise, elegant, and appropriate mathematical language

MATHEMATICAL REPRESENTATIONS

Sources of Evidence

a. Graphs, labels, charts

b. Models

c. Diagrams

d. Manipulatives

Final Rating

1. No use of mathematical representations

2. Use of mathematical representations

3. Accurate and appropriate use of mathematical representations

4. Perceptive use of mathematical representations

CLARITY OF PRESENTATION

Sources of Evidence

a. Audio or video tapes (or transcripts)
b. Written work
c. Teacher interviews or observations
d. Journal entries
e. Student comments
f. Student self-assessment

Final Rating

1. Unclear (disorganized, incomplete, insufficient detail)
2. Some clear parts
3. Mostly clear
4. Clear

SCORING RUBRIC

A scoring rubric identifies and gives a value to the different levels of respones to an open-ended question. Responses are sorted into piles according to three categories: (1) demonstrates competence; (2) satisfactory response, and (3) inadequate response. Each response is then reviewed and given a point value specified within each category. Papers in the first category may receive a point value of 5 or 6. In the second category the point values are 3 or 4, and in the last category the point values are 0, 1, or 2. The criteria for each rating are given below.

A Rating of 6

The response is complete with a clear and coherent explanation. The response includes an appropriate diagram or chart, identifies all the important elements of the problem, shows the relevant mathematical ideas and processes, and presents a strong supporting argument.

A Rating of 5

The response is reasonably clear. It may contain an appropriate diagram or chart and show some understanding of the mathematical ideas and processes. In addition, the response identifies most of the important elements of the problem.

A Rating of 4

The explanation has minor flaws, but is satisfactory. Some of the arguments may be incomplete or the response may be a bit unclear. The student may also have been ineffective in his/her use of diagrams or charts.

A Rating of 3

The response has serious flaws, but is almost satisfactory. The student begins the problem correctly, but fails to complete it or may omit significant parts of the problem. The student may make flagrant computation errors, use inappropriate terminology or symbolism, or use an inappropriate strategy for solving the problem.

A Rating of 2

The individual has started to solve the problem, but is unable to complete it. The explanation is not understandable and there is no evidence that the problem situation was completely understood.

A Rating of 1

The student was unable to begin the problem effectively. Parts of the problem are copied, but without working toward a solution.

A Rating of 0

The student made no attempt to solve the problem.

Each question or project needs to have its own rubric. The rubric needs to identify the goals and the expectations the teacher has for that particular question, so the teacher must create his/her own scoring rubric.

A scoring rubric can be created before or after reviewing some of the responses. If created before, allowances will need to be made for unusual responses. Creating the rubric after viewing a sampling of the responses may help in identifying the different levels. Either way, a scoring rubric needs to reflect what you, the teacher, values.

Creating and using a scoring rubric can be time consuming at first. To get started, work with a colleague. Working with another teacher to create the rubric and review the papers will increase your confidence in the consistency of grading. If you use the same question or project each year, save the rubric to use again, making adjustments as needed.

As your use of rubrics increases and you become more familiar with them, the amount of time spent grading holistically will decrease. Grading may still take longer than before, but the amount of information you receive from your students will also be greater.

SAMPLE RUBRIC

The rubric below was created for the following question.

Construct a table that shows several solutions of the equation $y = |x| + 1$. Then plot the corresponding points and describe the graphical pattern.

A Rating of 6

Student has constructed a table of several solutions to the equation, including x values that are positive and negative. The points are plotted correctly. A description of a V-shaped graph with its point at (0,1) is clearly stated.

A Rating of 5

Student has constructed a table of several solutions of the equation including x values that are positive and negative. The points are plotted correctly, but the description is curved instead of V-shaped.

A Rating of 4

The student has constructed a table of several solutions, however, only positive (or negative) x values were used. The points are plotted correctly, but the graphical pattern is described as a line.

A Rating of 3

The response is missing a part of the problem: (1) the table is not constructed, (2) the solution points are not plotted, (3) the solution points are plotted incorrectly, (4) the graphical pattern is not described.

A Rating of 2

Construction of the table is started. Some points are plotted, but they do not correspond to any points from the table.

A Rating of 1

The outline of a table is made, but no solutions are entered.

A Rating of 0

Student made no attempt to do the problem.

WHAT IS A PORTFOLIO?

Basically, a portfolio is a collection of work completed by an individual. Professionals such as artists, writers, and models use portfolios to demonstrate their best work. In mathematics, portfolios can be used to document a student's development. When using portfolios as a means of assessment, it is important to show what the student can do, rather than what the student cannot do. A mathematical portfolio is more than just a folder of a student's work; it can be used to gain insight into the student's mathematical reasoning, understanding, ability to communicate mathematically, and attitudes.

CONTENTS

Work in portfolios might include any or all of the following.

1. Open-Ended Questions, Problems, and Tasks   The student is given an open-ended question, a problem, or a task to discuss in writing. The student is asked to formulate hypotheses, explain a mathematical situation, make generalizations, and so on.

2. Research Projects   The student is given a long term project that requires use of resources outside the classroom. A time line is useful to keep students on track. The time line should include dates when the following are due: list of resources, outline, rough draft, and final project.

3. Presentations, Discussions, and Debates   The student writes a summary of the presentation, discussion, or debate including the original assignment, the outcome, and a list of resources used in researching the topic. The names of partners should also be listed.

4. Journal Entries   A journal entry consists of a student's writings about mathematics. These writings could include reflections and reactions about particular assignments or class activities.

5. Cooperative Learning Activities   The student writes his or her own summary of the work accomplished in the cooperative learning activity. The names of others in the group should be included.

6. Demonstrations   Demonstrations can be done in groups, pairs, or individually, and usually involve such tools as manipulatives, graph paper, compasses, calculators, or computers.

7. Math Logs   Math logs are worksheets that contain writing activities correlated to the lessons.

8. Investigations   The student keeps a log that includes the date, a description of the work done, and any questions to the teacher the student may have. The teacher's response to the question is written in the log.

9. Photographs   Items that are too bulky to fit into a portfolio can be photographed and the photograph included in the portfolio.

10. *Models and Simulations*   The student writes a summary that includes the original assignment and an explanation of the model or simulation. Diagrams, sketches and/or photographs should be included.

11. *Problem Solving*   A portfolio can contain the solutions of non-routine problems solved using the following five steps.

    • Read the problem. Be able to restate it in your own words.

    • Explore the problem, draw a picture, make charts, make diagrams.

    • Choose a strategy such as guess and test, look for a pattern, logical deduction, reduction, simulation, working backwards, and exhaustive listing.

    • Carry out the strategy and solve the problem.

    • Look back. Ask yourself, Is there another strategy I could have used to solve the problem? Is this a unique solution? Can I make a generalization? What if . . . (extend the problem)?

12. *Interviews*   During an interview, students talk about a problem they are solving while the teacher listens and asks questions. Students may be interviewed individually or in groups. Some examples of phrases used to encourage students to further elaborate on their explanations are as follows.

    • I am interested in your thinking.

    • Please help me to understand. Let's suppose that you are the teacher, and I am your student.

    • Sometimes when I am having trouble with a problem, I break it down into small steps. Let's try to do that now.

    • I understand it better now, but . . .

    • I like it when you take time to think about the problem and your explanation.

    Notes taken from the interview by the teacher or another student of the group may be included in the portfolio.

13. *Time-Staggered Sampling*   The portfolio can contain the results of work dealing with the same mathematical idea sampled at different times.

14. *Awards and Prizes*   The portfolio can contain descriptions or copies of awards and prizes that the student has won.

SPECIAL FEATURES

The following special features should be included in each student's portfolio: (1) table of contents, (2) identification of who selected the piece of work, (3) dates on all work, (4) description of the problem or task, (5) cover letter, and (6) comment sheet including self-assessment.

SELECTION PROCESS

Both the teacher and the student should have input into the selection process. The teacher may decide how many pieces are to be included, and the categories from which these pieces are to come. The student would then be allowed to choose the pieces, and have a comment sheet explaining how and why each of the pieces was chosen.

WHAT IS AN ERROR NOTEBOOK?

An error notebook gives students an opportunity to analyze and to learn from their errors.

To make an error notebook, follow the steps below.

1. Divide a notebook page into three columns as shown.

2. The first column should contain the problem on which the errors were made. The source (homework, quiz, or test) of the problem should also be included.

3. The second column should display exactly the error that was made. Draw a sad face next to the error to highlight the error that was made. The student might also include a statement such as "I drew a blank on this one," as an explanation of what went wrong. You might wish your students to use red ink for this column since this is the real source of the student's learning experience.

4. The third column should contain comments. The corrected problem should be displayed, including any thoughts or concepts that pertain to the problem.

5. Separate the problems with horizontal lines. Do not restrict the length of any column. Allow the students to write as much as they feel is necessary.

6. Students should spend a few minutes each day reading the notebook.

SAMPLE FORM

NAME_____		ERROR NOTEBOOK
Problem	**Error**	**Correction & Comment**
1. (Quiz on Oct. 20) A new bike costs $159.25, plus 6% sales tax. How much is your sales tax?	$159.25 × 0.6 = $95.55	$159.25 × 0.06 = $9.555 sales tax = $9.56 The decimal form of 6% is 0.06, not 0.6 which is the decimal form of 60%.
2.		

**WHAT IS A
MATH JOURNAL?**

A math journal can be used by students to assess their own progress in the course and to assess their attitude about the course.

You can ask students to complete journal entries on a regular basis (daily or weekly), or on an occasional basis. The questions used for the journal are up to you. The following sample is one that has been used by teachers on a daily basis.

SAMPLE FORM

DATE _____ M T W R F   Math Journal

1. What were the goals of today's math lesson?

   _____
   _____
   _____
   _____

2. Why did I learn this?

   _____
   _____
   _____

3. What strategies can I use to accomplish today's goals?

   _____
   _____
   _____

4. What did I like best about today's math class?

   _____
   _____
   _____

5. What was most frustrating about today's class?

   _____
   _____
   _____

**WHAT IS A
NOTEBOOK QUIZ?**

A notebook quiz is a one-page quiz that can be used as a substitute for collecting and grading notebooks. This gives students constant access to their notebooks while giving the teacher feedback on the completeness of the students' notebooks. Grading can be done over a period of a few days because the students retain possession of their notebooks.

If used, notebook quizzes should be given in class regularly. Students may use their notebooks to answer the questions, but may not use their textbooks or any other sources. Students should be told at the beginning of the course what type of information they need to keep in their notebooks. For instance, they should record dates, goals, definitions, and so on. Students also need to know that they are responsible for obtaining notes that were missed due to absence.

Here is a sample of the type of questions you might consider giving on a notebook quiz.

SAMPLE FORM

NOTEBOOK QUIZ   NAME _____

                                                                   DATE _____

1. What is the name of the chapter we have been studying?

2. State the goals discussed in class on January 27.
   Goal 1:
   Goal 2:

3. Define the term ratio.

4. State one of the goals discussed in class on January 31.

5. Given a fraction, explain how you can write an equivalent fraction.

6. State one of the goals discussed in class on February 2.

7. Complete the statement. A fraction is simplified if its numerator and denominator have no common factors other than _____.

8. What is the difference between a ratio and a proportion?

WHAT IS A DAILY QUIZ?

The teacher can use the daily quiz to determine if students need additional help or are ready for enrichment activities. If the class has a firm understanding of a topic, then less classroom time is needed for review and can instead be used in developing new concepts.

A daily quiz also provides the teacher with opportunity to assess the students' understanding of the previous day's lesson and homework assignment. The students are encouraged to prepare for the quiz by paying attention in class and completing the homework assignment.

THE DAILY QUIZ

Four problems should be on the chalkboard or the overhead so that the students can begin the quiz as soon as they enter the classroom. Students can grade each other's papers and keep them in their notebooks to be turned in on Friday, or the teacher can collect and distribute the papers daily. If each problem is worth 5 points, then the daily quizzes total 100 points by the end of the week.

SAMPLE FORM

An $8\frac{1}{2}$ by 11 sheet of paper can be divided into five rows and five columns. The first column lists the days of the week. The remaining four columns are for the four problems given each day.

Name _____ Class _____			
Monday			
Tuesday			
Wednesday			
Thursday			
Friday			

WHAT IS A PROJECT?

A project is an undertaking that requires effort over time. In this booklet, projects are divided into many headings: Research Project, Journal Entry, Construction, Demonstration, Interview Assessment, Problem Solving, Math Game, Cooperative Learning, Open-ended Question, and Discussion/Journal Entry. The projects can be used to extend the lesson, to provide an opportunity to observe your students, or to give students added insight into the algebra and geometry of the world.

Any of the projects can and should be adapted to your classroom. A construction problem could become a demonstration done by a group of students for the rest of the class. An open-ended question could lead to a group discussion. Students can make a journal entry to assess their attitudes and feelings about a completed project.

GRADING

Students should be aware of the grading criteria of a project when the project is assigned. If a scoring sheet is to be used, pass out a copy to the students so they are aware of the value of each portion of the assignment. Once graded, a project can be a wonderful addition to a student's portfolio.

Problem Solving Together

| COOPERATIVE LEARNING | *(Use after Lesson 1.1)*

1. Divide the class into groups of six.

2. Give each group a tape measure.

3. Give each group the following questions:

   a. Estimate the number of people it would take to fill the bleachers at your school's gymnasium.

   b. A regulation football field, from end line to end line, is 360 ft × 160 ft. Estimate the number of people that could stand on a football field.

   c. The Grand Canyon is 217 miles long. Estimate how many people it would take to stretch across this distance if the people were holding hands with their arms stretched as far as possible.

4. Have each group write up a description of how they would answer the given questions using only the group members, tape measure and a calculator. Have them answer the questions.

5. Have each group present their results to the class.

6. Have the class discuss any similarities or differences in their answers.

Assessment Goals:

- Develop estimation skills

- Develop problem-solving skills

| JOURNAL ENTRY/DISCUSSION | *(Use after Lesson 1.2)*

An arithmetic sequence is a list of numbers in which the next number in the list is found by adding a fixed number. For example, 2, 6, 10, 14, 18, 22 is an arithmetic sequence. Each number in the list is four greater than the previous number. The list of numbers that Gauss was asked to add was also an arithmetic sequence. Use the arithmetic sequence above and make up three more arithmetic sequences of your own. Determine whether or not Gauss' method, discussed in Lesson 1.2, for adding a list of numbers works for all four sequences.

Assessment Goals:

- Develop problem-solving skills

| COOPERATIVE LEARNING | *(Use after Lesson 1.6)*

1. Divide the class into groups of four.

2. Give each group a notepad, 60 second timer (minute glass), and a deck of cards with the face cards removed.

3. Begin the game by writing the number 25 on the notepad.

4. A student draws a card from the deck. If the card is black, the student must solve the equation $x +$ (number on the card) = (number on the notepad). If the card is red, the student must solve the equation $x -$ (number on the card) = (number on the notepad). For example, if the notepad has the number 25 and a student draws a 10 of hearts, he/she must solve $x - 10 = 25$.

5. The student has 60 seconds to find the solution. If correctly solved in the allotted time, the student may keep the card. Otherwise the card is placed at the bottom of the deck.

6. The number on the notepad changes with each correct play. The notepad number is the solution to the previous problem. This number should be clearly marked on the notepad for all the players to see. Any old numbers should be crossed out.

7. Play continues until all of the cards in the deck are gone.

8. The student with the most cards at the end of the game wins.

Assessment Goals:

- Develop equation solving skills

OPEN-ENDED QUESTION   *(Use after Lesson 1.7)*

Venn diagrams are often used in a branch of mathematics called set theory. Below are definitions of two terms from set theory. Use these definitions and Venn diagrams to answer the given questions.

DEFINITIONS:

The symbol for a subset is $\subseteq$. If one set of objects is a subset of another set of objects, every item in the first set is also an item in the second set.

The symbol for intersection is $\cap$. The intersection of two sets of objects contains all of the objects that belong to both sets.

QUESTIONS:

1. Give an example of a set of objects that is a subset of another set. Use a Venn diagram to illustrate your example.

2. When surveyed, 30 people said they own a dog, 20 people said they own a cat, and 5 people said they do not own either type of animal. Shade in the area on the Venn diagram that represents the intersection of the set of dog owners and cat owners. In words, describe what this intersection represents.

Assessment Goals:

- Expand mathematics vocabulary

- Develop skills in using Venn diagrams

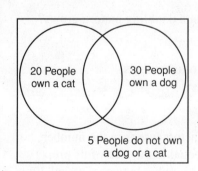

20 People own a cat

30 People own a dog

5 People do not own a dog or a cat

Number Relationships and Fractions

OPEN-ENDED QUESTION   *(Use after Lesson 2.1)*

Have the students insert the symbols, $+$, $-$, $\times$, $\div$, and parentheses in the boxes so that the equation is true.

a. $2 \ \square \ 3 \ \square \ 4 \ = \ 10$

b. $\square \ 4 \ \square \ 3 \ \square \ 3 \ \square \ 7 \ = \ 3$

c. $8 \ \square \ \square \ 3 \ \square \ 1 \ \square \ = \ 4$

d. $2 \ \square \ 4 \ \square \ 5 \ \square \ 3 \ \square \ = \ 10$

e. $3 \ \square \ 9 \ \square \ \square \ 2 \ \square \ 1 \ \square \ = \ 6$

Assessment Goals:

- Develop an understanding of the order of operations

DEMONSTRATION   *(Use after Lesson 2.2)*

1. Ask the class to vote on the answers to the following question: Would you rather be given a penny on Jan. 1 and every day after that double the amount of money you received the previous day until Jan. 31, or be given $10,000,000 on Jan. 31?

2. Have the class help you make a list of the money you would collect each day by doubling the money you receive.

3. Ask the class the following questions:

   a. What operation did you use to calculate each new number?

   b. Write a numerical expression for the amount you receive on Jan. 31 using exponents.

   c. Which method of payment was more profitable? Explain your answer.

   d. What does this tell you about how fast a doubling pattern grows?

Assessment Goals:

- Develop an understanding of the power of exponents

JOURNAL ENTRY   *(Use after Lesson 2.4)*

The proper factors of a number include all factors less than the number itself. A perfect number is a number that is equal to the sum of its proper factors. For example, $6 = 1 + 2 + 3$. Find a number between 20 and 30 that is a perfect number. Be sure to verify your results.

Assessment Goals:

- Develop skills in finding factors

1. Give each member of the class a 4 x 4 bingo card and several markers. The following are examples of bingo cards.

1	5	9	18
7	14	2	6
10	3	8	13
21	17	22	4

2	9	7	23
16	19	10	1
11	4	24	15
20	8	3	12

3	17	11	6
14	1	13	21
5	16	18	2
12	22	4	15

4	13	8	17
18	3	23	10
9	7	1	19
24	20	14	2

15	1	21	19
2	5	24	11
12	22	3	16
20	6	23	4

2. Have a bowl with slips of paper marked with pairs of numbers whose greatest common factors are 1–24. For example: 9 and 14; 18 and 20; 15 and 24; 24 and 44; 25 and 70; 18 and 48; 14 and 35; 8 and 64; 18 and 45; 30 and 50; 33 and 44; 24 and 36; 39 and 65; 28 and 70; 30 and 75; 32 and 48; 17 and 51; 36 and 90; 19 and 76; 40 and 100; 42 and 105; 44 and 66; 23 and 92; 72 and 96.

3. The students may place a marker on any number that is a common factor of the numbers drawn.

4. The first student to mark four numbers in a row, column, or on a diagonal wins the game. Be sure to verify the results based on the slips.

Assessment Goals:

• Develop skills in finding common factors

RESEARCH PROJECT   *(Use after Lesson 2.8)*

1. Divide the class into pairs.

2. Give each pair a research topic. Several examples are given below.

   a. Development of the computer

   b. Civil War

   c. History of the Chicago Bulls

   d. History of Flight

   e. U.S. Constitution and its Amendments

   f. History of Fashion

3. Have each pair research their topic at the library.

4. Have each pair construct a time line using events that they have determined (based on their research) are important to the topic.

5. Have each pair co-present a short oral report and explanation of their time line to the class.

Assessment Goals:

• Develop research skills

• Develop number-line construction skills

PROBLEM SOLVING   *(Use after Lesson 3.1)*

On Jan. 1, your school is going to host two basketball games. The boys' team plays at 6:00 P.M. and the girls' team plays at 8:30 P.M. During the month of January, the boys' team hosts a game every sixth day. The girls' team hosts a game every seventh day. Is it necessary to schedule another double game evening in January? Explain your reasoning. What if the girls' team played every fifth day? Explain your reasoning.

Assessment Goals:

- Develop skills in solving real-life problems

MATH GAME   *(Use after Lesson 3.3)*

1. Make a standard checker board.

2. In the squares write the following fractions:

$\frac{1}{2}$	$\frac{5}{6}$	$\frac{9}{7}$	$\frac{7}{6}$	$\frac{4}{5}$	$\frac{7}{10}$	$\frac{3}{2}$	$\frac{7}{3}$
$\frac{8}{9}$	$\frac{1}{10}$	$\frac{1}{8}$	$\frac{1}{4}$	$\frac{1}{11}$	$\frac{5}{8}$	$\frac{4}{9}$	$\frac{9}{4}$
$\frac{3}{5}$	$\frac{3}{11}$	$\frac{2}{3}$	$\frac{5}{12}$	$\frac{7}{9}$	$\frac{8}{5}$	$\frac{1}{6}$	$\frac{2}{7}$
$\frac{6}{5}$	$\frac{5}{11}$	$\frac{8}{11}$	$\frac{7}{5}$	$\frac{3}{8}$	$\frac{7}{12}$	$\frac{5}{3}$	$\frac{7}{11}$
$\frac{10}{3}$	$\frac{8}{3}$	$\frac{4}{7}$	$\frac{1}{12}$	$\frac{5}{7}$	$\frac{9}{8}$	$\frac{4}{11}$	$\frac{7}{4}$
$\frac{2}{9}$	$\frac{9}{11}$	$\frac{10}{7}$	$\frac{5}{9}$	$\frac{2}{11}$	$\frac{2}{5}$	$\frac{1}{9}$	$\frac{6}{7}$
$\frac{6}{11}$	$\frac{9}{2}$	$\frac{1}{5}$	$\frac{8}{7}$	$\frac{1}{7}$	$\frac{9}{10}$	$\frac{3}{7}$	$\frac{3}{10}$
$\frac{5}{2}$	$\frac{7}{8}$	$\frac{3}{4}$	$\frac{4}{3}$	$\frac{7}{2}$	$\frac{5}{4}$	$\frac{9}{5}$	$\frac{1}{3}$

3. This game is played by two students with the board above and 24 checkers. Each player gets 12 checkers (coins, beans, etc. may be used instead of checkers).

4. The game is played just like checkers with the following adjustments:

   a. Each time a checker is moved, the player must add the fractions on the original square and the new square.

   b. A player who wishes to "jump" a checker, must subtract the fractions on the starting and ending squares.

   c. A player who adds or subtracts incorrectly, loses his/her checker.

5. The game is over when one player has no more checkers.

Assessment Goals:

- Develop skills in adding and subtraction fractions.

In using the Distributive Property, we say that a is distributed over the sum $(b + c)$. That is $a(b + c) = ab + ac$. Can the Distributive Property be used over subtraction, $a(b - c) = ab - ac$? Multiplication, $a(b \cdot c) = ab \cdot ac$? Division, $a(b \div c) = ab \div ac$? Give examples or counterexamples for your conclusions.

Assessment Goals:

• Student discovery of properties of numbers.

CONSTRUCTION   *(Use after Lesson 3.7)*

Demonstrate the following division model for fractions. Use the examples $\frac{1}{4} \div \frac{1}{3}$ and $\frac{1}{2} \div \frac{1}{6}$.

1. Draw the area model for $\frac{1}{4} \div \frac{1}{3}$.

   a. Divide a unit square horizontally into thirds and vertically into fourths as in the diagram at the left.

   b. Write X's in one third of the unit square's rectangles as in the diagram at the left.

   c. Write O's in one fourth of the unit square's rectangles. Instead of marking these rectangles in a vertical column, overwrite as many rectangles with X's as possible as in the diagram at the left.

   d. What fraction of the rectangles with X's also have O's? $\frac{3}{4}$

2. Draw the area model for $\frac{1}{2} \div \frac{1}{6}$.

   a. Divide a unit square horizontally into sixths and vertically into halves.

   b. Write X's in one sixth of the unit square's rectangles.

   c. Write O's in one half of the unit square's rectangles. Instead of marking these rectangles in a vertical column, overwrite as many rectangles with X's as possible.

   d. What fraction of the rectangles with X's also have O's?

3. Have the students use this division model for the following exercises:

   a. $\frac{2}{3} \div \frac{1}{5}$

   b. $\frac{4}{5} \div \frac{1}{3}$

   c. $\frac{1}{2} \div \frac{3}{4}$

Assessment Goals:

• Develop skills in dividing fractions by using a visual technique.

1a.

1b.

1c.

Algebra and Integers

RESEARCH PROJECT *(Use after Lesson 4.2)*

1. Divide the class into pairs.

2. Give each group a piece of tracing paper, a red pen, tape, and a map of the United States. If you prefer, you can have the pairs go to the library and find a U.S. map.

3. Have the pairs draw a coordinate plane on the tracing paper. The unit marks should be an appropriate length based on the map's key. For example, for a key that indicates each $\frac{5}{4}$ inch is 1000 miles a unit could be 500 miles or $\frac{5}{8}$ inch. Be sure that all pairs use the same units.

4. Have each pair tape their coordinate plane to their map so that the intersection of the 20° latitude and 120° longitude lines are at the origin.

5. Have each pair locate three cities and assign each an ordered pair. Note that approximations may be necessary.

6. Create a large coordinate plane, as indicated above and a larger version of the U.S. map. Note that in your copy of the coordinate plane, the unit marks should be scaled to match those of the students' planes. This may be done on a bulletin board or on an overhead projector.

7. Have each pair mark their cities and ordered pairs on the large map.

8. Variations of this project can include using Canadian and Mexican cities, using maps of different world locations, or marking other important locations such as volcanoes or mouths of major rivers

Assessment Goals:

• Develop point plotting skills

• Show a connection between geography and mathematics

MATH GAME *(Use after Lesson 4.4)*

1. Make two number cubes out of foam. Write the numbers 1 through 6 on the faces of one number cube with a black marker. Write the numbers −1 through −6 on the faces of the other number cube with a red marker.

2. Divide the class into groups of four. Give each group a positive and negative number cube.

3. Give each member of the group a token. A checker or a coin work well.

4. Have each member of the group draw a number line from −20 to 20.

5. Each student begins by placing the token at 0.

6. The students take turns rolling the number cubes. The numbers rolled are added. Each student then adds that value to the number on which his/her token is currently sitting.

7. The first student to go past 20 wins.

8. A student who goes beyond -20 is out of the game.

Assessment Goals:

- Develop integer addition skills

| JOURNAL ENTRY | *(Use after Lesson 4.6)*

Read the following details about the 1996 World Series. Then answer the questions by writing and solving addition equations. *(Source: Information Please Almanac, Atlas and Yearbook, 1997)*

In the 1996 World Series, the New York Yankees beat the Atlanta Braves after six games (the World Series is a best of seven series). In game 1, Andruw Jones of Atlanta became the youngest player to hit a home run in the World Series. He was one year younger than the previous record holder, Mickey Mantle, who hit a home run in the 1951 World Series at the age of twenty. In fact, Jones hit his home run on what would have been Mantle's sixty-fifth birthday.

In game 2, Atlanta's first baseman, McGriff came to bat three times, got two hits, and received credit for three RBI's (runs batted in). Ultimately, Atlanta won the game four to zero.

In game 3, New York used four pitchers. The relievers, Rivera, Lloyd, and Wetteland pitched a total of three innings. Of Atlanta's six hits, Rivera gave up two. Atlanta did not score with Lloyd and Wetteland on the mound.

In game 4, a total of fourteen runs were scored. New York scored eight of these runs.

New York went on to win both game 5 and game 6. These wins made the New York Yankees the 1996 World Series champions. The Yankees have won more World Series than any other team. From 1903 to 1996, there have been ninety-two series. The Yankees have played in thirty-four series and have won twenty-three times!

1. In the 1996 World Series, how many games did not need to be played?

2. How old was Andruw Jones when he beat Mickey Mantle's record as the youngest player to hit a home run in a World Series game?

3. In game 2, how many of Atlanta's runs were not batted in by their first baseman, McGriff?

4. In game 3, how many innings did New York's starting pitcher, Cone, pitch?

5. In game 3, how many hits did Cone give up?

6. In game 4, how many runs did Atlanta score?

7. In the history of the World Series through 1996, how many times did the New York Yankees make it to the series only to lose?

8. How many times have the Yankees not been part of the World Series?

Assessment Goals:

- Develop skills in solving addition equations

- Develop skills in turning word problems into equations

| COOPERATIVE LEARNING | *(Use after Lesson 5.1)*

1. Divide the class into pairs.

2. Give each pair the following sets of data:

   a. 4, 4, 4, 5, 5, 7, 8, 8, 8, 9, 9, 10, 10, 10, 10

   b. 23, 24, 25, 30, 32, 32, 40, 41, 43, 43, 43, 44, 44, 45, 49

   c. 1, 2, 68, 69, 70, 70, 70, 81, 93, 94, 94, 95, 100, 102, 105

   d. 4, 4, 5, 7, 8, 9, 10, 10, 12, 12, 12, 13, 15, 79, 108

3. Have the pairs find the median and mean for each set of data.

4. Have the pairs determine for which sets of data the median is the best measure of central tendency.

5. Have the pairs theorize why the median is a better representation of these sets of data.

6. Have the pairs test their theory by creating a set of data that they believe will be best represented by the median. Then have them find the mean and median to verify their theory.

Assessment Goals:

- Develop an understanding of the use of means and medians

| JOURNAL ENTRY/DISCUSSION | *(Use after Lesson 5.2)*

Look in old newspapers and magazines that can be cut up. Find an example of a histogram, cut it out, and tape it to a blank sheet of paper. Below the histogram, write a short paragraph that interprets the information given in the histogram.

Assessment Goals:

- Show relationship between mathematics and interpreting real-life data

| COOPERATIVE LEARNING | *(Use after Lesson 5.5)*

1. Divide the class into groups of three.

2. Have each group decide upon an interview question to ask their class-mates. Some sample questions are given below.

   a. What is your favorite food?

   b. How many siblings do you have?

   c. What is your favorite school subject?

3. Have each group submit their question so that it can be checked for appropriateness and to be sure that there are no duplications.

4. Once each group's question has been submitted and approved, the groups are responsible for collecting the data from the class.

5. Have each group create a bar graph that represents their data.

6. Post the various graphs around the room.

7. Give each student a worksheet with questions that ask them to interpret the various bar graphs. The questions you ask depend upon the information gathered by your class. Some examples include:

   a. What type of food is the most popular among your classmates?

   b. Approximately how many people in your class are only children?

   c. What is the most popular school subject among your classmates?

Assessment Goals:

• Develop skills in creating and interpreting bar graphs

DEMONSTRATION   *(Use after Lesson 5.7)*

1. Put 60 marbles in a large jar: 13 red, 12 green, 18 blue, and 17 yellow marbles. Tell the students that there are 60 marbles in the jar, but do not reveal how many of each color.

2. Perform an experiment in which students randomly choose one marble from the jar, returning it to the jar.

3. Set up a frequency table to indicate how many times a marble of each color is chosen.

4. Have the students determine the probability that the marble chosen is red. Repeat this process for green, blue, and yellow marbles.

5. Have the students estimate how many red, green, blue, and yellow marbles are in the jar by using the definition of probability and the Guess, Check, and Revise method.

6. Empty the jar and count the number of red, green, blue, and yellow marbles.

7. Have the students discuss the following questions:

   a. How accurate were your answers?

   b. Explain why your answers may have been incorrect.

Assessment Goals:

• Develop an understanding of probabilities

• Use problem-solving techniques from earlier lessons to solve current problems

---

| COOPERATIVE LEARNING | *(Use after Lesson 6.1)*

1. Divide the class into groups of four.

2. Give each group a ruler, string, and a compass.

3. Give the groups the following definitions:

   a. A diameter of a circle is a segment that begins and ends on the circle and passes through the center of the circle.

   b. A radius of a circle is a segment from any point on the circle to the center. Thus a diameter has twice the length of a radius.

   c. The circumference of a circle is the distance around the circle.

4. Demonstrate the use of a compass for drawing circles.

5. Demonstrate how to read the compass to determine the length of a radius of a circle drawn by a compass.

6. Have each member of the group draw a circle with the compass and determine the length of a diameter of their circle.

7. Have each member of the group measure the circumference of their circle by placing the string around the circle and measuring the length of the string with the ruler.

8. Have each member of the group find the ratio of the circumference to the diameter and write this fraction as a decimal.

9. Have the group members compare their results. Have the groups write a general rule about the ratio of any circle's circumference and diameter.

10. Have the groups come together as a class and compare their results. Inform the class that this ratio is the number π.

Assessment Goals:

- Introduce the number π, as is relates to ratios

- Develop construction, measuring, and ratio skills

| JOURNAL ENTRY | *(Use after Lesson 6.2)*

Give each student a section of a newspaper or magazine. Have the students divide a sheet of paper into two columns. Title the first column RATIOS and the second column RATES. Have the students read through their material and write down any examples of ratios and rates that they find. Have them include a brief explanation of the ratio or rate. For example, on the sports page, a student may find 3.2 as an earned run average for a pitcher. This means that a pitcher has allowed an average of 3.2 runs to score per nine innings that he has pitched. This is an example of a rate.

Assessment Goals:

- Develop an appreciation for the variety of uses of ratios and rates in real-life applications

COOPERATIVE LEARNING   *(Use after Lesson 6.6)*

1. Divide the class into groups of four.

2. Have the groups construct three different pairs of similar triangles.

3. Have the groups measure the sides of each pair of similar triangles and verify that their corresponding sides are proportional.

4. Have the groups determine the perimeter of each triangle. Based on the results of the three different pairs, find a relationship between the ratios of the perimeters of similar triangles and the ratios of their corresponding sides.

5. The area of a triangle is defined as half the base times the height.

6. Find the areas of the triangles at the left and write a ratio of the areas. Then compare this ratio to the ratios of the corresponding sides.

7. How are these ratios related to each other?

8. Have the groups test their theory by examining the ratios of the areas of their three pairs of similar triangles. Note that for comparison, it may be easier to examine the ratios in decimal form.

Assessment Goals:

- Discovery of properties of similar triangles

$$A = \tfrac{1}{2} bh$$

RESEARCH PROJECT   *(Use after Lesson 6.7)*

1. Divide the class into pairs.

2. Allow each pair to choose from a list of research topics. Some examples are given below.

   a. Solar System

   b. Boeing 747

   c. Golden Gate Bridge

   d. Saturn

   e. The inner layers of the earth

   f. Capitol building

   g. White House

3. Have each pair research their topic to find the dimensions of its major features.

4. Have the students create a model for their topic.

5. The models may take the form of a scale drawing or a three-dimensional model made of clay, cardboard, or any medium in which the pair wish to work.

6. Along with each project, have the students include a card stating the scale factor they used along with life-sized measurements.

Assessment Goals:

- Develop skills in using scale factors and proportions

JOURNAL ENTRY *(Use after Lesson 7.2)*

Have each student bring in three different receipts for items that are taxed. Grocery, restaurant, gas station, and some department store receipts work well. Have each student verify that the computer correctly computed the tax and total for the items based on your state's tax rate. Have each student explain how he/she arrived at their answers and explain any rounding methods used by the state.

Assessment Goals:

• Demonstrate the use of percents in everyday life

COOPERATIVE LEARNING *(Use after Lesson 7.2)*

1. Divide the class into groups of four.

2. Give each group an example of a restaurant bill. The example can either be an actual bill or a made up example. If you create the bill make sure you include all typical items such as the prices of the meals and the tax as well as a line for the customer to include a tip and a total line.

3. Inform each group that it is customary to leave a 15% tip for the waiter/waitress if the service was good.

4. Have the group determine how much money should be left for a 15% tip.

5. Give the groups the following short cut techniques for estimating a 15% tip:

   METHOD 1: Use the total, slide the decimal one place to the left and call that number A, find half of A and add it to A. The sum is 15% of the original number.

   METHOD 2: Find the line that tells you how much tax was paid and use the states tax rate to help you estimate 15%. For example if your state has a 7% tax, then double that amount for approximately a 15% tip. In this case, your answer gives a 14% tip.

6. Have the groups discuss the two techniques and explain why they work.

7. Have the groups determine which method they prefer and explain why.

Assessment Goals:

• Develop skills in finding and estimating percents of a number

1. Divide the class into groups of four.

2. Assign each group a topic. Sample topics are given.
   a. Clubs
   b. Family
   c. Music
   d. Pets
   e. School
   f. Sports

3. Have each group make up two questions for their topic. The questions should be such that the answers can be given in one word (not yes/no). The group must have their questions approved by the teacher before proceeding.

4. Have each group collect data regarding their survey questions from the class.

5. Have the groups organize their data in two bar graphs using percents.

6. Have each group create one question per graph that can be answered by knowing the class size and looking at their graphs.

7. Create a worksheet using the students' questions.

8. Post all of the graphs around the room.

9. Have the students individually answer the questions on the worksheet.

Assessment Goals:

- Develop skills in solving percent equations

- Develop skills in creating and reading graphs

JOURNAL ENTRY *(Use after Lesson 7.5)*

Keep a record of all the money that you spend for one week. The record should include the amount spent as well as the item. At the end of the week, list your expenditures under one of the following categories:
   a. School supplies
   b. Food (anything not supplied at home)
   c. Entertainment
   d. Clothes
   e. Miscellaneous

Make a circle graph for your weekly expenditures using percents to label the graph.

Assessment Goals:

- Develop skills in working with percents

- Develop graph construction skills

COOPERATIVE LEARNING *(Use after Lesson 8.2)*

1. Divide the class into groups of four.

2. Give the groups the following explanation: When a figure is reflected in the *x*-axis, every point on a figure jumps across the *x*-axis such that the vertical distance from the original point to the *x*-axis is equal to the vertical distance from the reflected point to the *x*-axis. For example,

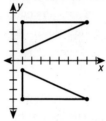

If you fold the coordinate plane along the *x*-axis, the two figures will lie on top of each other.

3. Have the groups discuss and answer the following questions about *x*-axis reflections:

   a. If a triangle has vertices (1, 3), (–2, 4), and (2, 5), what are the vertices of the triangle reflected in the *x*-axis?

   b. In general, how are the coordinates of a point changed when it is reflected in the *x*-axis?

4. Have the groups discuss and answer the following questions about *y*-axis reflections:

   a. Draw an example of a figure that is reflected in the *y*-axis.

   b. Where must you fold the coordinate plane in order for the figures to lie on top of each other?

   c. If a triangle has the vertices (1, 1), (3, –2), and (5, 1), what are the vertices of the triangle reflected in the *y*-axis?

   d. In general, how are the coordinates of a point changed when it is reflected in the *y*-axis?

Assessment Goals:

• Extend connections between the geometry and algebra of congruent figures

1. Divide the class into groups of four.

2. Give the groups the following scenario and have them answer the questions. For the championship basketball game, the pep club is planning on making a large hoop banner for the team to break through as they enter the court. In order to construct such a banner several items must be considered.

3. To determine the diameter of the banner, have the groups answer the following questions:

   a. Estimate the maximum height of the basketball player that will run through the banner. Why is this information important?

   b. Should the diameter of the banner be equal to or greater than the height of the tallest player? Explain your answer. If you believe the diameter should be greater than the height of the tallest player, how much greater?

   c. What about the distance across the banner? Does this distance need to be greater than the height? Explain your answer. How will this affect the diameter?

   d. The cheerleaders need to hold the banner upright. You will need some wire around the edge of the banner to make it stiff. Estimate how much extra length you need to add to the diameter of the circle to account for the wire.

   e. Estimate the total diameter of the banner.

4. To determine how much paper you need to buy, have the groups answer the following questions:

   a. Draw a sketch showing a square piece of paper with as big a circle as possible sketched on it.

   b. Since you do not want to waste paper, what will be the relationship between the diameter of the circle and the width of the paper?

   c. What do the dimensions of the piece of paper need to be?

   d. Estimate how much paper will be wasted.

5. To determine the amount of wire needed to put around the edge of the banner, have the groups answer the following questions:

   a. Into what shape will you bend the wire?

   b. What word from Chapter 8 did you learn that describes the length of the wire?

   c. Estimate how much wire is required.

Assessment Goals:

- Develop students' ability to plan a construction that entails several geometric ideas

- Develop students' understanding of circles, circumference, and area

| **CONSTRUCTION** | *(Use after Lesson 9.1)*

1. Divide the class into groups of four.

2. Give each group a bunch of pipe cleaners of at least two different lengths.

3. Have each group construct an example of the following type of polyhedrons by using the pipe cleaners as the edges of the polyhedron:

   a. Triangular prism

   b. Rectangular pyramid

   c. Prism with different side lengths

   d. Pyramid with equal side lengths

   e. Polyhedron that is neither a prism nor a pyramid

Assessment Goals:

• Develop students' ability to recognize and construct polyhedrons

| **COOPERATIVE LEARNING** | *(Use after Lesson 9.2)*

1. Divide the class into groups of four.

2. Provide each group with a set of 27 blocks. Assume each block has the dimensions 1 unit x 1 unit x 1 unit.

3. Have the groups build as many different rectangular prisms as possible. Note that a 27 x 1 x 1 prism is the same as a 1 x 27 x 1 prism and a 1 x 1 x 27 prism.

4. Have the groups determine the surface area of each prism.

5. Have the groups determine which prism has the smallest surface area.

6. Repeat steps 3–5 using 8 blocks.

7. Have the groups discuss and answer the following question: If the same number of blocks are used to construct rectangular prisms, what type of prism gives the smallest surface area?

8. Have the groups discuss this question if a cube cannot be built from the given number of blocks. For example, repeat steps 3–5 and answer the question from step 7 using 18 blocks.

Assessment Goals:

• Develop students' skills in finding the surface area of rectangular prisms

• Develop generalization skills

COOPERATIVE LEARNING   *(Use after Lesson 9.4)*

1. Provide the class with a box filled with various nuts, bolts, nails, screws, etc.

2. Have each member of the class randomly select one of the objects from the box.

3. Have each student draw a top, front, and side view of the object.

4. Divide the class into groups of six.

5. Have the six group members mix up their objects.

6. Have each group member take a turn at showing their drawings.

7. Have the other group members determine which object is represented by the set of drawings.

Assessment Goals:

• Develop students' spatial visualization skills

COOPERATIVE LEARNING   *(Use after Lesson 9.7)*

1. Divide the class into groups of four.

2. Give each group the following definition: Two cylinders are similar if their corresponding dimensions (radius and height) are proportional.

3. Have the groups draw two different pairs of similar cylinders.

4. Have the groups find the surface area of each cylinder.

5. Have the groups find the ratio of surface areas of similar cylinders.

6. Have the groups generalize how the ratio of surface areas of similar cylinders relates to the ratio of corresponding dimensions of similar cylinders.

7. Have the groups find the volume of each cylinder.

8. Have the groups find the ratio of volumes of similar cylinders.

9. Have the groups generalize how the ratio of volumes of similar cylinders relates to the ratio of corresponding dimensions of similar cylinders.

Assessment Goals:

• Develop students' ability to find surface area and volume of cylinders

• Develop students' ability to discover other geometric relationships based on known relationships

| COOPERATIVE LEARNING | (*Use after Lesson 10.6*)

1. Bring in the following items to class:
   a. one head of lettuce, shredded
   b. one medium tomato, sliced
   c. one medium onion, sliced
   d. 1 lb sandwich meat
   e. 1 lb cheese, sliced
   f. one bottle of salad dressing and a small measuring device
   g. one package of submarine sandwich buns

2. Divide the class into seven groups. Assign each group an ingredient.

3. Inform each group of the price of their item. The price may be given in terms of a unit price or a price per pound.

4. Have the groups answer the following questions:
   a. How many submarine sandwiches can be prepared with the ingredients your group was given?
   b. Your goal is to sell 80 submarine sandwiches. How much of your ingredient do you need to purchase? Keep in mind that you cannot buy half a head of lettuce, however, you can be a little more exact when buying lunch meat.
   c. How much will it cost to purchase the total quantity of your ingredient for 80 submarine sandwiches?

5. Have the groups come together and report their findings by filling in the appropriate information on the chart pictured below.

EXPENSES	UNIT PRICE	UNITS	TOTAL
lettuce			
tomato			
onion			
meat			
cheese			
salad dressing			
buns			
TOTAL:			_____

6. Have the class as a whole, discuss and answer the following questions:
   a. If the class charges $1 per submarine sandwich, how much money will be earned or lost?

b. How much money should be charged per submarine sandwich so that the class breaks even?

c. If the class wishes to earn $160, how much profit should they earn per submarine sandwich?

d. How much money should be charged per submarine sandwich to reach this $160 profit goal?

Assessment Goals:

- Develop multiplication and division skills

COOPERATIVE LEARNING *(Use after Lesson 10.8)*

1. Divide the class into groups of four.

2. Provide the groups with the following information:
The metric system is a base 10 system of measurement. This means that all of the units of measure for a particular quantity are based on a power of ten of a basic unit. For example, the meter (m) is the basic unit of length. However, length can be measured in terms of centimeters (cm) and kilometers (km). One centimeter is 1×10^{-2} meters. One kilometer is 1×10^3 meters. Different prefixes are used to represent different powers of 10. The table below shows several prefixes and their notation.

Prefix	Factor of 10	Symbol	Prefix	Factor of 10	Symbol
giga	10^9	G	centi	10^{-2}	c
mega	10^6	M	milli	10^{-3}	m
kilo	10^3	k	micro	10^{-6}	μ
hecto	10^2	h	nano	10^{-9}	n

3. Have the groups discuss and answer the following questions:

a. What is the symbol for a gigameter?

b. What unit of measure is symbolized by μm?

c. Write 1 mm in terms of meters. Which is a better representation of the length? Explain your answer.

d. How many meters are in a megameter? If an object has a length of 2 Mm, is it better to represent the length in terms of megameters or meters? Explain your answer.

e. An object has a width of 3,200 m. What metric unit would be a more appropriate unit of measure? Convert the width to this unit of measure.

f. An object has a height of 0.00000000472 m. What metric unit would be a more appropriate unit of measure? Convert the height to this unit of measure.

Assessment Goals:

- Develop skills in using powers of ten

- Explore the connection between powers of ten and the metric system

| MATH GAME | *(Use after Lesson 11.2)*

1. Divide the class into groups of four.

2. Give each group the following items:

   a. A jar with 4 red balls, 2 yellow balls, and 1 green ball

   b. A stack of note cards with a variety of color combinations written on them (1 red, 1 yellow, 1 green, 2 red, 1 red and 1 green, 2 yellow, etc.)

   c. The following game board:

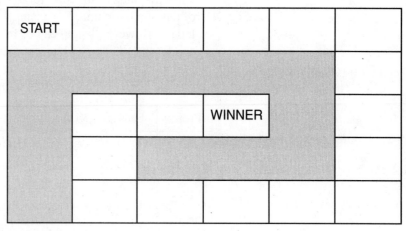

   d. A marker for each player

3. Have each student take a turn at drawing a card.

4. After reading the card, have the student decide whether he/she wants to risk 0, 1, 2, or 3 places on the board.

5. After the student makes their risk selection, have them randomly select the total number of balls indicated on their card.

6. If their selection matches the description on the card, they move their marker ahead the number of spaces that they risked.

7. If their selection does not match the description on the card, they must move their marker back the number of spaces that they risked.

8. The markers cannot be moved backward any farther than the original START position.

9. Have the group members take turns until someone reaches the WINNER space.

Assessment Goals:

• Develop students' ability to use counting techniques and probability

(Use after Lesson 11.4)

1. Divide the class into groups of five.

2. Have the groups perform the following exercises:

   a. Select two people from the group to form a subgroup. Have each person in the subgroup shake hands with every other subgroup member. How many hand shakes were there?

   b. Repeat exercise a using 3, 4, and 5 people in the subgroup.

   c. Do these exercises involve counting permutations or combinations? Explain your answer.

   d. How many hand shakes would there be among 6 people? 7 people?

Assessment Goals:

- Develop counting skills

- Develop ability to recognize the difference between permutations and combinations

RESEARCH PROJECT *(Use after Lesson 11.6)*

1. Divide the class into pairs.

2. Assign each pair a stock to follow in the Wall Street Journal. Make this paper available to the class on a daily basis during this project.

3. Have the pairs record the number of days in one work week in which the price of the stock went up.

4. Have the pairs predict how many times in the next 10 work days that the stock will rise.

5. Have the pairs follow their stock for an additional ten days to see if their prediction came true.

6. As a class, discuss possible reasons why a stock may have done better or worse than the students predicted.

Assessment Goals:

- Develop students' ability to predict events

- Show how mathematics is related to real-life problems

JOURNAL ENTRY   *(Use after Lesson 12.1)*

The invitation to a friend's birthday party included directions to her house from Main St. Travel south on Main St., turn left at the first light onto Jackson St., go up a steep hill and turn right onto Azalea Dr., at the second stop sign, turn left onto Rose Dr. The house is the second house on the right. Give directions for getting back to Main St.

Assessment Goals:

- Develop skills in using inverse operations

COOPERATIVE LEARNING   *(Use after Lesson 12.5)*

1. Divide the class into pairs.

2. Give each pair a hanger balance. To construct the hanger balance follow the steps outlined below.

   a. Connect a string to opposite sides of a paper cup.

   b. Tie the strings to the bottom of the hanger. Make sure the string is secure on the hanger. Slipping will cause the balance to be inaccurate.

   c. In the same way, connect a second cup to the other side of the hanger.

3. Give each pair a stack of dominoes and some rubber bands.

4. Have one student use the rubber bands to make stacks of dominoes. He/she may make as many stacks as he/she wishes, but all stacks must have the same number of dominoes. How many dominoes in a stack is up to the student.

5. The student then places his/her stacks plus any number of single dominoes in one of the cups of the hanger balance.

6. The student then writes an expression that represents what has been placed in the cup. For example, if there are two stacks and four single dominoes, the expression is $2x + 4$.

7. The second student fills the empty cup with single dominoes until a balance is achieved.

8. This student then writes an equation that represents the condition of the balance. For example, if 8 single dominoes creates a balance, the equation is $2x + 4 = 8$.

9. This student then solves the equation and tells the first student how many dominoes were in his/her stack(s).

10. Have the students take turns reversing their roles each time.

Assessment Goals:

- Develop equation solving skills

JOURNAL ENTRY   *(Use after Lesson 12.6)*

1. Provide access to a clock with a second hand.

2. Have each student find his/her pulse on their wrist or neck.

3. Have the students count the number of beats in 10 seconds.

4. Have the students create a function in which the input is time in seconds and the output is beats. This function can be created using a proportion.

5. Have the students make a scatter plot for their function.

6. Have the students use their function to determine the number of beats in 30 seconds and 60 seconds.

7. Have the students test their function by counting the number of beats in 30 seconds and 60 seconds and comparing the results to those obtained from their function.

Assessment Goals:

- Develop skills in creating functions that model real-life conditions

---

COOPERATIVE LEARNING   *(Use after Lesson 12.6)*

1. Divide the class into groups of four.

2. Give each group the following items: teaspoon, tablespoon, cup, water, ruler, and metric ruler.

3. Have the group experiment with their objects and write functions for the following relations:

    a. Find the number of tablespoons for a given number of teaspoons.

    b. Find the number of cups for a given number of tablespoons.

    c. Find the number of teaspoons for a given number of cups.

    d. Find the the number of inches for a given number of centimeters. Note that this will be an approximation.

Assessment Goals:

- Develop skills in seeing relationships between quantities and writing these relationships as functions

WHAT ARE PARTNER QUIZZES?

Partner quizzes are used not only to assess students' achievement, but also to encourage students to communicate mathematically with each other. Copymasters for Mid-Chapter Partner Quizzes are provided on pages 39-50. They correspond in content to the Mid-Chapter Self-Tests in the student's text and to the Mid-Chapter Tests in the *Formal Assessment* copymasters. Here are two ways to use partner quizzes.

FIRST WAY

Three copies of the *same* quiz are given to two students. For the first ten minutes, each person works independently, answering as many of the questions as possible. The two students are then allowed to work together as partners. During this time, they are to complete the third copy of the quiz. The two partners turn in only the third copy, which shows the answers and work that they have agreed upon.

This type of quiz emphasizes the importance of mathematical communication. A student whose answers differ from his or her partner's needs to be able to explain how he or she approached the problem and also to explain the reasoning used to make each decision. Students need to recognize that there is often more than one correct approach to solving a problem. The partners then need to decide which approach they will submit on the third copy of the quiz. A student who develops a mental block on a problem can benefit from having his or her memory jogged by a partner.

SECOND WAY

Another way to give students a partner quiz is to have one problem written on the overhead. One student (the interpreter) in each pair faces the overhead and the other (the solver) faces away from the overhead. Ask each interpreter to silently read and interpret the problem. After a couple of minutes, turn off the overhead. Each interpreter then explains the problem to his or her solver. The solver must then use the information given by the interpreter to solve the problem. After the interpreter has explained the problem, he or she must remain quiet. The interpreter cannot help his or her partner solve the problem. Therefore, it is important for the interpreter to do a good job explaining the problem and giving all of the relevant information. The partners may then switch roles and continue with the next problem or they may wait until the next quiz to switch roles.

This type of activity emphasizes the importance of reading the problem, and then interpreting the information. It also helps to teach students to differentiate between information needed to solve the problem and extra information.

1. A stack of thirty sheets of paper is about $\frac{1}{8}$ of an inch thick. A ream of paper is about $\frac{5}{3}$ inches thick. How many sheets of paper are there in a ream?

   1. _____

2. The measurements of a model car are $\frac{1}{10}$ the measurements of the real car. The width of the model is $\frac{4}{5}$ feet. What is the width of the car?

   2. _____

3. How many different rectangles whose sides are measured in whole inches have an area of 20 in.²? A rectangle that measures 3 in. x 5 in. is the same as one that is 5 in. x 3 in.

   3. _____

4. A pizza shop offers 12 different toppings. In how many different ways can you order two toppings?

   4. _____

5. Determine a pattern for the square numbers below. Find the 12th square number.

   5. _____

6. Complete the statement using *always*, *sometimes*, or *never*. Squares are ? similar.

   6. _____

7. Which figure is similar to ?

   7. _____

   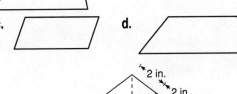
   a.   b.   c.   d.

8. Find the perimeter and area of the figure.

   8. _____

9. Use an experiment to determine how many times it would take to toss a coin to have two heads in a row?

   9. _____

10. In a game you are asked to choose a number from 1 to 6. You play the game twice. Name an item that could be used to simulate the chance of choosing the numbers 3 and 5.

    10. _____

1. Insert parentheses to make the statement true.
   $2 + 3 \times 6 = 30$

   1. _____

2. Evaluate the expression $18 \div (10 - 4) \times 2$.

   2. _____

3. Evaluate $7 + 2x$ when $x = 3$.

   3. _____

4. Write the product $w \cdot w \cdot w \cdot w \cdot w \cdot w \cdot w$ as a power and evaluate when $w = 2$.

   4. _____

5. Write a formula for the volume of the given cube.

   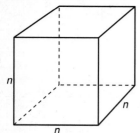

   5. _____

6. Complete the statement using $>$, $<$, or $=$.
   4^2 $\boxed{?}$ 4×2

   6. _____

7. Find a number that is divisible by 2, 3, and 5.

   7. _____

8. Find the missing digit that makes $14{,}34\,\boxed{?}$ divisible by 3 and 4.

   8. _____

9. Write the prime factorization of 360.

   9. _____

10. Complete the statement using *always*, *sometimes*, or *never*. Composite numbers are $\boxed{?}$ even.

    10. _____

1. List the first 5 multiples of 3 and 5. Find the least common multiple.

    1. _____

2. Complete the statement using *always, sometimes,* or *never*. The least common multiple of two different prime numbers is $\boxed{?}$ their product.

    2. _____

3. Rewrite $3\frac{2}{7}$ as an improper fraction.

    3. _____

4. Complete the statement using *always, sometimes,* or *never*. A proper fraction can $\boxed{?}$ be written as a mixed number.

    4. _____

5. Rewrite $\frac{14}{3}$ as a mixed number.

    5. _____

6. Find the difference. $\frac{2}{3} - \frac{1}{5} - \frac{1}{4}$

    6. _____

7. Use Mental Math or the Guess, Check, Revise strategy to determine what fraction of students surveyed prefer rye bread.

    7. _____

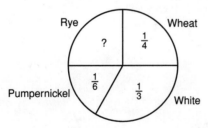

8. Simplify the mixed number. $3\frac{7}{4}$

    8. _____

9. Find the difference. $4\frac{1}{3} - 2\frac{1}{2}$

    9. _____

10. Find the perimeter of the given rectangle.

    10. _____

$3\frac{2}{5}$ in.

$8\frac{1}{4}$ in.

1. Write an expression that represents the pattern: When m is 0, the value of the expression is -2. Each time m increases by 1, the value of the expression increases by 7.

1. _____

Use the following scenario to answer Exercises 2 and 3. It costs $20 per month for basic cellular phone service plus 30¢ for each minute of calling time.

2. Write an expression that represents your monthly cellular phone costs for x minutes of calling.

2. _____

3. What is your cost if you spent 10 minutes on the phone during February?

3. _____

4. Write the ordered pair that is represented by A.

4. _____

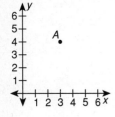

5. Draw a scatter plot that represents the equation $y = 3x - 2$. Use x-values of 1, 2, and 3.

5. _____

6. Which number is less, -1000 or 3?

6. _____

7. Complete the statement using *always, sometimes,* or *never.*
   Zero is ? smaller than a negative number.

7. _____

8. Complete the statement using *always, sometimes,* or *never.*
   The sum of a positive and a negative number is ? positive.

8. _____

9. Use a number line to find $-3 + 4 + (-2)$.

9. _____

10. Write the keystrokes you would use on a calculator to solve $4 + (-6)$. Then solve.

10. _____

| **Chapter 5** **Mid-Chapter Partner Quiz** | *(Use after Lesson 5.4)* | Names _____ _____ |

Use the following data to answer Exercises 1–3.

10, 10, 11, 11, 12, 13, 15, 16, 16, 16, 19, 23, 25, 25

1. Find the mean of the data.

2. Find the median of the data.

3. Find the mode of the data.

1. _____

2. _____

3. _____

Use the following data to answer Exercises 4 and 5. The data below shows test scores out of a possible 100 points for 20 students:

80	75	68	92	88
73	82	77	83	81
61	87	86	71	90
95	74	91	52	74

4. Make a frequency table for this data using the intervals: 0-9, 10-19, 20-29, 30-39, 40-49, 50-59, 60-69, 70-79, 80-89, 90-99.

5. Draw a histogram of the data.

6. When drawing a box-and-whisker plot, do you use the mean, median, or mode to find the first, second, and third quartiles?

7. Draw a box-and-whisker plot for the data.
   1, 2, 4, 8, 9, 12, 12, 14, 15

8. Plot the points (–2, –3), (–1, 4), and (2, –2) on a coordinate plane.

9. Write the ordered pair that represents A.

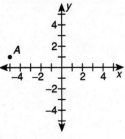

10. What do the ordered pairs of all points that do not lie in a quadrant have in common?

4. _____

5. _____

6. _____

7. _____

8. _____

9. _____

10. _____

1. Write the ratio of the shaded area to the area of the entire region.

   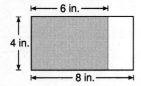

   1. _____

2. Complete the quotient so that it can be written as a ratio. Then rewrite the quotient as a ratio.

   $$\frac{8 \text{ cm}}{11 \boxed{?}}$$

   2. _____

3. A 16 oz bottle of shampoo costs \$2.89. A 32 oz bottle costs \$4.98. Which is the better bargain?

   3. _____

4. A serving of raisins has 124 calories that come from 31 grams of carbohydrates. Find the unit rate.

   4. _____

5. Solve the proportion. $\dfrac{8}{7} = \dfrac{x}{56}$

   5. _____

6. The ratios of the dimensions of a model plane to the real plane is $\dfrac{1}{12}$. If the wing span of the plane is 36 ft, what is the wing span of the model?

   6. _____

7. Write the description as a proportion and solve the proportion.
   n is to 15 as 5 is to 3.

   7. _____

8. Use cross products to solve the proportion. $\dfrac{1.3}{x} = \dfrac{4}{5}$

   8. _____

9. Use the cross product property to complete the statement. If $\dfrac{r}{s} = \dfrac{w}{y}$, then _____.

   9. _____

10. If you travel at a constant rate of 60 miles per hour, how long does it take you to travel 300 miles?

    10. _____

1. Write 32% as a fraction and a decimal.

    1. _____

2. Write $\frac{7}{9}$ as a percent. Round your answer to one decimal place.

    2. _____

3. 36% of 1200 is what number?

    3. _____

4. A survey asked 120 people what type of movie was their favorite. The results are shown in the circle graph below. How many people preferred dramas?

    4. _____

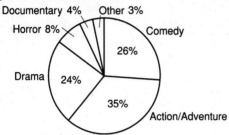

Documentary 4%   Other 3%
Horror 8%
Comedy 26%
Drama 24%
35%
Action/Adventure

5. Complete the statement with *always*, *sometimes*, or *never*. If you find less than 1% of a number, the answer is ⏹? less than 1.

    5. _____

6. Complete the statement with *always*, *sometimes*, or *never*. If you find greater than 100% of a number, the answer is ⏹? greater than the original number.

    6. _____

7. Complete the statement using <, >, or =.

   $\frac{1}{4}$% of 20,000 ⏹? 120% of 20

    7. _____

8. In a machine shop, 1% of the pieces produced are defective. If you receive a shipment of 500 parts how many will have a defect?

    8. _____

9. What percent of questions did you answer correctly if you correctly answered 23 out of 25 questions.

    9. _____

10. In a survey, 120 people said that they exercised twice a week. If this represented 48% of the people surveyed, how many people were asked?

    10. _____

1. Name all angles in the figure that are congruent to ∠1.

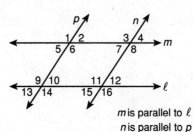

m is parallel to ℓ
n is parallel to p

1. _____

2. Complete the statement using *always, sometimes, or never.* If two lines are intersected by a third line, corresponding angles are ⟨?⟩ congruent.

2. _____

3. Name all of the angles in the figure congruent to ∠1.

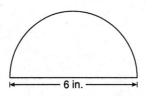

3. _____

4. The coordinates of a figure are A(3, 1), B(4, 4), and C(5, –3). The coordinates of its translation are D(0, –1), F(1, 2), and G(2, –5). Describe the translation.

4. _____

5. Complete the statement using *always, sometimes, or never.* When a figure is translated in the plane, the translated figure is ⟨?⟩ congruent to the original figure.

5. _____

6. The radius of a circle is 6 in. Find the circumference of the circle.

6. _____

7. Find the perimeter of the semi-circle at the right.

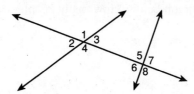

├──── 6 in. ────┤

7. _____

8. Find the area of the parallelogram at the right.

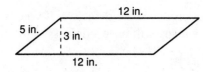

12 in.
5 in.
3 in.
12 in.

8. _____

9. Find the missing measure.
A = 58 sq m

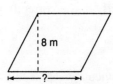

8 m
?

9. _____

10. Complete the statement using *all, some, or no.* ⟨?⟩ parallelograms are squares.

10. _____

1. Complete the following statement. The base of a pyramid can be any type of polygon; however, all other faces must be $\boxed{?}$.

    1. _____

2. A particular polyhedron has 6 faces and vertices. How many edges does it have?

    2. _____

3. Complete the statement using *all, some, or no*. $\boxed{?}$ polyhedrons can be classified as a prism or a pyramid.

    3. _____

4. Find the surface area of the prism below.

    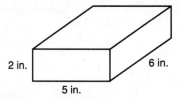

    2 in.   6 in.

    5 in.

    4. _____

5. What is the surface area of a cube without a top face and dimensions 4 cm x 4 cm x 4 cm?

    5. _____

6. Find the surface area of a cylinder with diameter 16 in. and height 20 in.

    6. _____

7. Complete the following statement. The lateral surface area of a cylinder equals the product of the $\boxed{?}$ of the circular base and the height of the cylinder.

    7. _____

8. Which cylinder has the greater surface area?
    Cylinder A: radius = 2 in.   height = 3 in.
    Cylinder B: radius = 3 in.   height = 2 in.

    8. _____

9. What type of polyhedron has the same top, side, and front views?

    9. _____

10. Draw the top, front, and side views of the given solid.

    10.

1. Complete the statement using *always, sometimes,* or *never.* The absolute value of a number is ⟨?⟩ equal to the absolute value of the number's opposite.

   1. _____

2. Complete the statement using *always, sometimes,* or *never.* The absolute value of a number is ⟨?⟩ positive.

   2. _____

3. Evaluate $|-2.76|$.

   3. _____

4. Complete the statement using $<$, $>$, or $=$.
   If $a < b$ and $b < 0$, then $a + b$ ⟨?⟩ 0.

   4. _____

5. Evaluate $3 + (-14)$.

   5. _____

6. Complete the following statement. Subtracting -7 from 3 is the same as adding _____.

   6. _____

7. Evaluate $-3 - 6$.

   7. _____

8. Complete the statement using *always, sometimes,* or *never.* The y-values of the scatter plot of $y = |x|$ are ⟨?⟩ negative.

   8. _____

In Exercises 9–10, use the following table of values.

x	-3	-2	-1	0	1	2	3
y	6	4	2	0	2	4	6

9. Make a scatter plot of the data.

   9.

10. Complete the statement using *smaller than, larger than,* or *equal to.* The angle created by the graph of the data is ⟨?⟩ the angle created by the graph of $y = |x|$.

    10. _____

1. What is the probability of rolling an even number on a number cube?

   1. _____

2. On average, a certain baseball player gets a hit 2 out of 5 times at bat. What is the probability that he will get a hit? Is this an experimental or theoretical probability?

   2. _____

3. You can be in one of the following language clubs: French, Spanish, or Russian. You can be in one of the following publishing clubs: News-paper or Yearbook. Use a tree diagram to count the number of club choices.

   3. _____

4. The zip code of your friend's address is 152 [?] [?] . What is the proba-bility of guessing the last two digits correctly?

   4. _____

5. There are four members on a swimming relay team. In how many different orders can they swim?

   5. _____

6. If you are a member of a three person relay team, what is the probability that you will run the last leg of the race?

   6. _____

7. In how many ways can you order a 10 question quiz?

   7. _____

8. Complete the statement using *is* or *is not*. When listing combinations, order [?] important.

   8. _____

9. Count the number of combinations of choosing 2 people from 3.

   9. _____

10. If 2 people are to be elected from a group of 3, what is the probability that you and your friend are elected?

    10. _____

1. Describe the inverse operation of the operation given below.

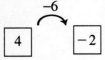

1. _____

2. Solve the equation by using an inverse operation.
   $-2x = 8$

2. _____

3. What is the inverse operation of dividing by -7?

3. _____

4. Solve the equation $m - (-4) = 7$.

4. _____

Use the following information to answer Exercises 5–7. You have a 10 dollar bill to take to the movies. A ticket costs $6, a small popcorn costs $1.50, and a small drink costs $1.

5. Use the verbal model below to write an equation.

   [_____] + [_____] = [_____]

5. _____

6. How much change do you receive after buying the ticket?

6. _____

7. How much change do you receive if you then buy a small popcorn and a small drink?

7. _____

8. What operation do you use to solve a multiplication equation?

8. _____

9. Solve the equation $-3w = -21$.

9. _____

10. The circumference of a circle is 16π in. What is the radius of the circle?

10. _____

**WHAT IS
GROUP ASSESSMENT?**

Students learn from each other when they work together. In a small group setting, students are better able to share their ideas while exploring a problem, developing a strategy to solve the problem, and then solving the problem. Assessment should be part of this learning activity; it provides insight into the thought process of the students.

The goal of the group assessment in this supplement is not to grade the students on the solution. The goal is to assess (1) their understanding of the problem, (2) how they solve the problem, and (3) how well they work together in a small group.

The blackline masters for group assessment can be found on pages 52–75 of this supplement. There are two pages for each chapter. The first page is an activity or a problem for a group of three or four students to explore. The second page is a similar activity or problem for the individual to explore. The individual page should motivate students to participate and work to understand the group activity.

GRADING

There are two ways to assign grades to the students. The group and individual pages are scored and each member of the group receives the sum of the points on the group page and their individual page. Alternatively, the group and individual pages are scored and each member of the group receives the sum of the points on the group page and the average of the individual pages of the members of the group. When using the second grading option, students will often make a greater effort in the group setting to insure that every person understands the problem and the solution.

Materials: A number cube and a spinner

Explore: A granola company has announced a contest. The company has stamped one of the letters Y, E, and S on the inside of each granola bar wrapper. If you collect the letters YES, you receive a free poster. The chance in finding the Y is twice that of finding the S. The chance in finding the E is three times that of finding the S. How many granola bars do you expect to buy to collect YES?

1. Discuss possible strategies for solving the problem. What strategy did the group select? Explain your answer.

2. What is the least number of granola bars you need to buy to win the poster?

3. How many granola bars do you expect to buy to win the poster?

4. If the chance of finding each letter was the same, would this increase or decrease the number of granola bars you expect to buy to win the poster?

Materials: A number cube and a spinner

Explore: A bubble gum company has announced a contest. The company
has stamped one of the letters Y, O, U, W, I, and N on the inside
of each package of gum. The chances of finding a vowel are
twice that of finding a consonant. If you collect the letters YOU
WIN, you receive a free package of gum. How many packages
of gum do you expect to buy to receive a free package?

1. Rewrite the problem in your own words.

2. Choose a plan for solving the problem. Explain why you made
this selection.

3. Did you use any information learned in the group activity to help
you solve this problem? If so, what was it?

4. What is the least number of packages of gum you need to buy?

5. How many packages of gum do you expect to buy to receive a
free package?

Materials: Calculator

Explore: There is a fraction that is equal to $0.\overline{3}$. How do you write this repeating decimal as a fraction?

1. Write an approximation of $0.\overline{3}$ using six decimal places.

2. Enter this number on your calculator and then multiply by 10. What is the result?

3. Since the number from question 1 is only an approximation of $0.\overline{3}$, what would you expect the product of 10 and $0.\overline{3}$ to be?

4. What is the difference when you subtract $0.\overline{3}$ from $10 \times 0.\overline{3}$?

5. If you replace $0.\overline{3}$ with the variable y in question 4, you get the equation $10y - y = \boxed{?}$. Replace the $\boxed{?}$ with your answer for question 4 and solve the equation.

6. Since you replaced $0.\overline{3}$ with y, $0.\overline{3}$ is equal to what fraction?

7. What fraction is equal to $0.\overline{5}$?

Materials: Calculator

Explore: There is a fraction that is equal to $0.\overline{23}$. How do you write this repeating decimal as a fraction?

1. How is this problem different from the problem discussed in the group activity?

2. What did you learn from the group activity that will help you develop a strategy for solving this problem?

3. Write a procedure for finding the fraction that is equal to $0.\overline{23}$.

4. What fraction is equal to $0.\overline{23}$?

Materials: None

Explore: In Lesson 3.5, a step-saving technique referred to as cancellation was introduced. This technique involves dividing the numerator and denominator of two fractions by a common factor before finding the product. In the examples, only fractions in which the numerator of one fraction equaled the denominator of the other fraction were used. Can this method be extended to include fractions that do not have a common numerator and denominator?

1. Create a multiplication of fractions problem in which the numerator of one fraction and the denominator of the second fraction are the same. Demonstrate the cancellation technique.

2. How does the question you are asked to explore differ from the set-up in Question 1?

3. Develop a strategy for solving the problem.

4. Can the cancellation technique be used if one numerator and denominator are not the same? If so, explain when this occurs. If not, explain your reasoning.

5. Give two examples or counterexamples to illustrate your conclusions.

Materials: None

Explore: Can the cancellation technique described in the group activity be used to save steps when adding or subtracting two fractions in simplest form?

1. Rewrite the problem in your own words.

2. Develop a strategy for solving this problem.

3. What did you learn in the group activity that can help you solve this problem?

4. Can the cancellation technique be used in the addition or subtraction of fractions in simplest form? Explain your answer.

5. Give two examples or counterexamples to illustrate your conclusions.

Materials: None

Explore: Let a, b, c, and d be integers. If $a < b$ and $c < d$, what is the relationship between $a + c$ and $b + d$?

1. Rewrite the problem in your own words.

2. Discuss possible strategies for solving this problem. Which strategy did the group choose? Why?

3. What is the relationship between $a + c$ and $b + d$? Give your answer in words as well as in the form of an inequality.

4. Does this property of inequalities hold for any combination of positive integers, negative integers, or zero? If yes, give several examples. If no, explain why not.

Materials: None

Explore: Let *a, b,* and *k* be integers. If $a < b$, what is the relationship between $a + k$ and $b + k$?

1. Rewrite the problem in your own words.

2. What strategy will you use to solve this problem? Was it a strategy similar to that used by the group? If so, explain the similarities and differences. If not, explain why your strategy is better suited for the problem.

3. What is the relationship between $a + k$ and $b + k$? Write your answer in words as well as in the form of an inequality.

4. Does this property of inequalities hold if *a* and *b* are either positive integers, negative integers, or zero? Provide examples or counterexamples to support your answer.

5. Does this property of inequalities hold regardless of whether *k* is a positive integer, a negative integer, or zero? Provide examples or counterexamples to support your answer.

Materials: Graphing paper, ruler

Explore: In Lesson 4.2, you learned how to make a scatter plot from an equation. It is also possible to approximate an equation from a scatter plot. This equation can be used to approximate data that has not been given. Finding this unknown data is known as *interpolation*. The table below shows the profit or loss for a company after a number of years in business. Find an equation that approximates the profit or loss.

Years in Business	1	2	3	4	5
Profit/Loss (in $)	−350	−200	0	100	225

1. Draw a scatter plot for the data.

2. Sketch a line that approximates the given data.

3. The equation of a line has the form $y = \boxed{A}x + \boxed{B}$. Where does your line cross the *y*-axis? Substitute this value for $\boxed{B}$.

4. Put your pencil anywhere on the line. Move one unit to the right. Estimate how far up you have to move to get back on the line. Substitute this value for $\boxed{A}$.

5. Write an equation that approximates the given data.

6. Use this equation to approximate the profit/loss of the company after 1.5 years.

Materials: Graphing paper, ruler

Explore: *Extrapolation* is a technique in which you use given data to approximate what will happen beyond the data that is given to you. For example, you can approximate what will happen in the future based on the collected data. To do this you need to approximate the given data with an equation. The table below shows data for the the profit/loss of a company after a given number of years in business. Estimate the company's profit/loss after 10 years in business.

Years in Business	1	2	3	4	5
Profit/Loss (in $)	−100	−20	100	230	290

1. Draw a scatter plot for the data.

2. Sketch a line that approximates the given data.

3. What did you learn from the group activity that will help you find the equation of this line?

4. What is the equation of the line that approximates the given data?

5. Use this equation to approximate the profit/loss of the company after 10 years.

(Use after Lesson 6.5)

Names _____

_____

Materials: Calculator

Explore: The Golden Ratio is approximately 1.62, or $\frac{81}{50}$. When a line
segment is divided into two pieces whose ratio is the Golden
Ratio, it has the property that $(a + b)/a =$ Golden Ratio.

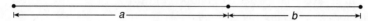

You are making a picture frame that has a height-to-width ratio
that is the Golden Ratio. You have a 16-ft piece of wood from
which to build the frame. What are the dimensions of the largest
frame you could build with this specification?

1. Draw a picture of the material you are given and the frame that you wish
to build. Label all known quantities and assign variables to all unknown
quantities.

2. Write a verbal model for the proportion such that the height-to-width
ratio of your frame is the Golden Ratio.

3. Write the proportion using your assigned variables and known quantities.

4. Find the height of the frame. Round your answer to two decimal places.

5. Find the width of the frame. Round your answer to two decimal places.

| Chapter 6 Individual Assessment | (Use after Lesson 6.5) | Name _____ |

Materials: Calculator

Explore: The Golden Ratio is approximately 1.62, or $\frac{81}{50}$. The given line segment is divided into two pieces whose ratio of lengths is the Golden Ratio. That is, a/b = Golden Ratio.

You are making a picture frame that has a height-to-width ratio that is the Golden Ratio. In order for the picture to fit, the frame must have a height of 3 ft. What is the total length of material needed to construct the frame?

1. Rewrite the problem in your own words.

2. Develop a plan for solving this problem.

3. How is this question different from the question asked in the group activity?

4. Write a proportion to find the width of the frame. Solve the proportion and round your answer to two decimal places.

5. What is the total length of material needed to construct the frame?

Materials: Calculator

Explore: Simple interest is not usually used when calculating amounts of loans. Calculating interest on loans is complicated by the fact that each month you must repay part of it. That means that the amount of interest you pay decreases each month. When you turn 16, you may want to buy a car. Your parents have agreed to cosign a loan at the bank. When you go to the bank to apply for your loan, you see the table below.

Auto Loan Repayment Options
(Per $1000 at 9% annual interest)

Number of Months	Payment Per Month	Total Amount Repaid
18	59.60	1072.80
24	45.69	1096.56
30	37.35	1120.50
36	31.80	1144.80
48	24.89	1194.72

1. If you wish to borrow $1000, how many months does the least expensive repayment option take?

2. If you can only afford to pay $50 per month, which payment option is the least expensive? Explain your answer.

3. How much money will you have to repay for a $1000 loan if you pay it off in 24 months? How much of this total is strictly interest?

4. How much would it cost you in interest to borrow $1000 and repay it in 36 months? 48 months?

5. The table can also be used for loan amounts other than $1000. For example to borrow $2000 for 18 months, your monthly payment would be 2 × 59.60, or $119.20. What would be the total amount repaid on a $2000 loan paid off in 18 months?

Materials: Calculator

Explore: It is deceiving how much interest you pay when you take
out a loan. In the group activity you discovered that a $1000
loan with an annual interest rate of 9% would cost you $96.56
in interest if you payed it back in 24 months. Using a credit card
is like taking a loan too. If you had a $1000 balance and your
credit card charged 18%, the table below shows how much it
would cost you to pay it off using different monthly payments.

Repayment of a $1000 balance
(18% interest)

Monthly Payment	Months Needed	Total Repaid
100	11	1092.19
75	15	1124.10
50	24	1198.08
25	62	1538.12

1. How much did it cost (interest) to borrow the $1000 from the credit card
company if you pay off the balance at $50 per month?

2. Find the difference in cost (interest) of the $1000 auto loan to the $1000
credit card balance when both are paid off in 24 months.

3. When you make smaller monthly payments, what happens to the total
repayment cost?

4. Write a statement about the total costs of borrowing money on credit
cards.

Materials: None

Explore: Using the concepts of measurement of angles from Lesson 8.1, describe the relationship between the opposite interior angles of a parallelogram.

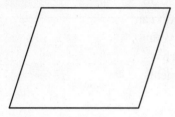

1. Rewrite the problem in your own words.

2. Redraw the given parallelogram so that the sides are extended into lines.

3. Discuss strategies for answering the question. Which strategy did your group select? Explain your answer.

4. What information from Lesson 8.1 did your group use?

5. What is the relationship between the measures of opposite interior angles of a parallelogram?

Materials: None

Explore: Using the concepts of the measures of angles from Lesson 8.1, is there a relationship between the opposite interior angles of a trapezoid?

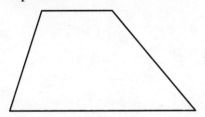

1. Rewrite the problem in your own words.

2. Develop a strategy for solving the problem.

3. What information from the group activity will help you answer this question?

4. Is there a relationship between the measures of opposite interior angles of a trapezoid? Explain your answer.

Materials: None

Explore: Find a pattern for the amount of concrete needed to build a concrete staircase with a given number of steps. Let each step have the following dimensions: width = 5 ft; length = 2 ft; height = 1 ft.

1. Draw pictures of a one step, two step, and three step staircase with the given dimensions.

2. What measure discussed in Chapter 9 will determine how much concrete is needed to build each staircase?

3. Discuss different strategies for finding a pattern for the amount of concrete needed to build a staircase with *n* steps. Choose a strategy. Why did the group select this strategy?

4. Describe the pattern for the concrete required to build a staircase with *n* steps of dimension 5 ft x 2 ft x 1 ft?

5. How much concrete is needed to build a staircase with 6 steps?

Materials: None

Explore: Find a pattern for the amount of carpeting needed to cover the fronts and tops to the steps of a staircase with *n* steps. Let each step have the following dimensions: width = 5 ft; length = 2 ft; height = 1 ft.

1. Explain why neither volume nor surface area is a correct measure for the amount of carpeting needed to cover the steps.

2. What measure will you use to determine the amount of carpeting needed to cover the staircase?

3. What strategy will you use to find a pattern in the amount of carpeting used to cover *n* steps?

4. Was the strategy you selected different from that of the strategy selected in the group activity? Explain your answer.

5. Describe the pattern for the amount of carpeting required to cover *n* steps.

6. How much carpeting is needed to cover a staircase with 6 steps?

Materials: Graph paper

Explore: Describe the pattern in a scatter plot of the absolute value equation $y = -|x|$.

1. Describe the pattern of the scatter plot of the absolute value equation $y = |x|$.

2. How does the equation $y = |x|$ differ from $y = -|x|$?

3. Discuss several strategies for solving this exercise. Which strategy did your group select? Why?

4. Describe the pattern of the scatter plot of $y = -|x|$.

5. Are there any points common to both $y = |x|$ and $y = -|x|$? Explain your answer.

6. Are the y-values of $y = -|x|$ all positive or zero, negative or zero, or zero and both positive and negative numbers? Explain your answer.

Materials: Graph paper

Explore: Describe the pattern in the scatter plot of the absolute value equation, $y = |-x|$.

1. How does this absolute value equation differ from $y = |x|$ and $y = -|x|$?

2. Consider several strategies for solving this exercise. Which strategy did you select? Why?

3. Describe the pattern in the scatter plot of $y = |-x|$.

4. How is this pattern related to the pattern of $y = |x|$?

5. Explain why the patterns of $y = |x|$ and $y = |-x|$ are related in the way you described in Exercise 4.

Materials: None

Explore: Find a formula for calculating the number of permutations of n objects grouped r objects at a time. The notation for this is $P_{n,\,r}$.

1. What is the formula for finding the number of permutations of n objects if each permutation includes all n objects? That is, n objects grouped n at a time.

2. Use the formula to find the number of permutations of A, B, C, and D if all four letters are used in each permutation. (This number is $P_{4,\,4}$.)

3. List the permutations of A, B, C, and D if only three of the letters are used. How many permutations of four letters grouped three at a time are there?

4. List the permutations of A, B, C, and D grouped two at a time. How many are there? List the permutations grouped 1 at a time. How many are there?

5. What integer could you divide by to go from $P_{4,\,4}$ to $P_{4,\,3}$? $P_{4,\,4}$ to $P_{4,\,2}$? $P_{4,\,4}$ to $P_{4,\,1}$?

6. Evaluate $(n - r)!$ for $n = 4$ and $r = 3$, 2, and 1. How are these numbers related to the values found in exercise 5?

7. Write a formula for finding the number of permutations of n objects grouped r objects at a time.

8. Test your formula by listing the permutations of A, B, and C taken two at a time and then using your formula.

| Chapter 11 Individual Assessment | *(Use after Lesson 11.4)* | **Name** _____ |

Materials: None

Explore: Find a formula for calculating the number of combinations of n objects grouped r objects at a time. The notation for the number of these combinations is $C_{n,\,r}$.

1. Use the formula found in the group activity to find $P_{4,\,4}$. Note that by definition, $0! = 1$.

2. List the combinations of A, B, C, and D grouped four at a time. How many are there? (This number is $C_{4,\,4}$.)

3. Find $P_{4,\,3}$. List the combinations of $C_{4,\,3}$. What is $C_{4,\,3}$?

4. Find $P_{4,\,2}$. List the combinations of $C_{4,\,2}$. What is $C_{4,\,2}$?

5. Find $P_{4,\,1}$. List the combinations of $C_{4,\,1}$. What is $C_{4,\,1}$?

6. In each case, what do you divide $P_{n,\,r}$ by to get $C_{n,\,r}$?

7. Use factorials to represent these numbers. How are they related to the number of objects in the group?

8. Write a formula for calculating $C_{n,\,r}$.

9. Test your formula by listing the combinations of A, B, and C grouped two at a time and then using the formula.

Materials: None

Explore: In Lesson 12.1, you studied inverse operations. In mathematics, you will also study inverse functions. The picture below illustrates what an inverse function does. How do you determine the equation used to represent an inverse function?

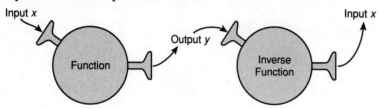

Input x   Output y   Input x

Function   Inverse Function

1. What does an inverse function do? (Refer to the diagram above.)

2. Based on the diagram and your answer to Exercise 1, what is the output of the inverse function shown below?

3   6   ?

Function   Inverse Function

3. Given the function $y = x + 3$, discuss and answer the following questions:

    a. What does the function do to the input?

    b. What will the inverse function do to its input?

    c. Write an equation that represents the inverse function. Let x represent the input and y represent the output.

4. Given the following functions, write the equation for the inverse function.

    a. $y = x + 2$ **b.** $y = x - 4$

    c. $y = x + \frac{1}{3}$ **d.** $y = x - 0.6$

Materials: None

Explore: How do you determine the equation used to represent an inverse function if the original function involves the multiplication or division operation. For example, find the inverse function of $y = 2x$.

1. In your own words, define an inverse function.

2. What did you learn from the group activity that will help you answer the given question?

3. What operation will be involved in the inverse function of $y = 2x$?

4. Write an equation for the inverse function of $y = 2x$.

5. Based on what you have learned, write an inverse function for each of the following functions.

   a. $y = 8x$ **b.** $y = \dfrac{x}{3}$

   c. $y = 0.4x$ **d.** $y = \dfrac{x}{2.1}$

Answers to Chapter Projects

■ Chapter 1

Cooperative Learning (Page 14)

Answers vary.

Journal Entry/Discussion (Page 14)

72; Answers vary; Gauss' method does work for adding the numbers in any arithmetic sequence.

Cooperative Learning (Page 14)

Games vary.

Open-Ended Question (Page 15)

1. Examples vary.

2.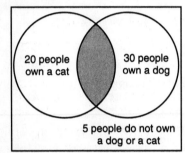

20 people own a cat

30 people own a dog

5 people do not own a dog or a cat

The intersection is the group of people that own both a dog and a cat.

■ Chapter 2

Open-Ended Question (Page 16)

a. $2 \times 3 + 4 = 10$

b. $(4 + 3)3 \div 7 = 3$

c. $8 \div (3 - 1) = 4$ or $8 - (3 + 1)$

d. $2 + 4(5 - 3) = 10$

e. $3 + 9 \div (2 + 1) = 6$

Demonstration (Page 16)

2. 0.01, 0.02, 0.04, 0.08, 0.16, 0.32, 0.64, 1.28, 2.56, 5.12, 10.24, 20.48, 40.96, 81.92, 163.84, 327.68, 655.36, 1310.72, 2621.44, 5242.88, 10485.76, 20971.52, 41943.04, 83886.08, 167772.16, 335544.32, 671088.64, 1342177.28, 2684354.56, 5368709.12, 10737418.24

3.a. Multiplication by 2.

b. $0.01(2)^{30}$

c. Doubling your money each day is more profitable. On Jan. 31 alone you receive over $10,000,000 and you have not yet added all of the money from the entire month.

d. A doubling pattern grows very quickly.

Journal Entry (Page 16)

$28 = 1 + 2 + 4 + 7 + 14$

Math Game (Page 17)

Games vary.

Research Project (Page 17)

Reports and time lines vary.

■ Chapter 3

Problem Solving (Page 18)

No, the least common multiple of 6 and 7 is 42. There are not 42 days in the month of January. However, the least common multiple of 5 and 6 is 30. Thus, there needs to be a double game scheduled on Jan. 30.

Math Game (Page 18)

Games vary.

Journal Entry (Page 19)

The Distributive Property can be used over subtraction, but not over multiplication and division. Examples and counterexamples vary.

Construction (Page 19)

3. a. $\frac{10}{3}$

b. $\frac{12}{5}$

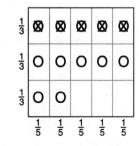

c. $\frac{4}{6} = \frac{2}{3}$

	$\frac{1}{2}$	$\frac{1}{2}$
$\frac{1}{4}$	⊗	⊗
$\frac{1}{4}$	⊗	⊗
$\frac{1}{4}$	X	X
$\frac{1}{4}$		

■ Chapter 4

Research Project (Page 20)

Answers vary.

Math Game (Pages 20 and 21)

Games vary.

Journal Entry (Page 21)

1. $x + 6 = 7$; $x = 1$ **2.** $x + 1 = 20$; $x = 19$

3. $x + 3 = 4$; $x = 1$ **4.** $x + 3 = 9$; $x = 6$

5. $x + 2 = 6$; $x = 4$ **6.** $x + 8 = 14$; $x = 6$

7. $x + 23 = 34$; $x = 11$

8. $x + 34 = 92$; $x = 58$

■ Chapter 5

Cooperative Learning (Page 22)

3.a. 7.4, 8   **b.** 37.2, 41   **c.** about 74.3, 81
   d. about 20.5, 10

4. c and d

5. The median is a better representation of a set of data in which a few pieces of data are much smaller or much larger than the rest of the data. These few elements will cause the mean to be artificially small or large.

6. Answers vary.

Journal Entry/Discussion (Page 22)

Answers vary.

Cooperative Learning (Pages 22 and 23)

Answers vary.

Demonstration (Page 23)

3. Frequency tables vary.

4. Probabilities vary but should be close to the following: red: $\frac{13}{60} \approx 0.22$; green: $\frac{12}{60} = 0.2$; blue: $\frac{18}{60} = 0.3$; yellow: $\frac{17}{60} \approx 0.28$

5. Answers vary but should be close to 13 red, 12 green, 18 blue, and 17 yellow.

6. 13 red, 12 green, 18 blue, and 17 yellow

7. Answers vary.

■ Chapter 6

Cooperative Learning (Page 24)

9. All of the ratios are approximately 3.14. The ratio of any circle's circumference to its diameter is approximately 3.14.

Journal Entry (Page 24)

Answers vary.

Cooperative Learning (Page 25)

2. Answers vary.   **3.** Measures vary.

4. Perimeters vary. The ratio of perimeters of similar triangles is the same as the ratio of their corresponding sides.

6. 486, 150, $\frac{81}{25}$

7. The ratio of the areas of similar triangles is the square of the ratio of their corresponding sides.

8. Ratios vary, but will always be the square of the ratio of the corresponding sides.

Research Project (Page 25)

Models vary.

■ Chapter 7

Journal Entry (Page 26)

Answers vary.

Cooperative Learning (Page 26)

4. Answers vary.

6. In METHOD 1, moving the decimal point one place to the left is the same as finding 10% of the total. Half of 10% is 5%. Thus the sum of 10% and 5% is 15%.

In METHOD 2, the tax in most states is 6% or 7%. By doubling the tax, you leave a 12% or 14% tip. If your tax rate is 6% you may wish to leave a little more than the tax doubled.

7. Answers vary.

Interview Assessment (Page 27)

Answers vary.

Journal Entry (Page 27)

Graphs vary.

■ Chapter 8

Cooperative Learning (Page 28)

3.a. (1, –3), (–2, –4), and (2, –5)

  b. The *y*-coordinate changes sign.

4.a. Examples vary.   **b.** Fold along the *y*-axis.

  c. (–1, 1), (–3, –2), and (–5, 1)

  d. The *x*-coordinate changes sign.

Cooperative Learning (Page 29)

3.a. Answers vary. This information is important because the banner must have a large enough diameter for the tallest player to run through.

  b. The diameter of the circle should be greater than the height of the tallest player because the player must fit through the hoop as he/she is running. A perfect fit is not safe. Answers vary.

  c. The width is not the critical measurement. An athlete will be taller than he/she is wide. The widths of the player will have no affect on the diameter of the circle. The largest length (height) will be used.

  d. Answers vary.   **e.** Answers vary.

4.a.

  b. The diameter of the circle and the width of the paper should be equal.

  c. Diameter × diameter

  d. $d^2 - \pi\left(\dfrac{d}{2}\right)^2$

5.a. Circle   **b.** Circumference   **c.** $\pi \cdot d$

■ Chapter 9

Construction (Page 30)

Polyhedrons vary.

Cooperative Learning (Page 30)

3. $27 \times 1 \times 1$
$9 \times 3 \times 1$
$3 \times 3 \times 3$

4. 110 square units
78 square units
54 square units

5. $3 \times 3 \times 3$

6. $8 \times 1 \times 1$; 34 square units
$4 \times 2 \times 1$; 28 square units
$2 \times 2 \times 2$; 24 square units
$2 \times 2 \times 2$ prism has the smallest surface area

7. Cubes yield the smallest surface area.

8. $18 \times 1 \times 1$; 74 square units
$9 \times 2 \times 1$; 58 square units
$6 \times 3 \times 1$; 54 square units
$3 \times 3 \times 2$; 42 square units
$3 \gtrsim 3 \times 2$ prism has the smallest surface area.
A cube made of 18 blocks is not possible.
However, the prism whose shape was closest to that of a cube had the smallest surface area.

Cooperative Learning (Page 31)

Drawings and answers vary.

Cooperative Learning (Page 31)

3. Answers vary.   **4.** Answers vary.

5. Answers vary.

6. (ratio of corresponding dimensions)² = (ratio of surface areas)

7. Answers vary.   **8.** Answers vary.

9. (ratio of corresponding dimensions)³ = (ratio of volumes)

■ Chapter 10

Cooperative Learning (Pages 32 and 33)

4. Answers vary.   **5.** Chart varies.

6. a. Answers vary.   **b.** Answers vary.

  c. $2   **d.** Answers vary.

Cooperative Learning (Page 33)

3. a. Gm   **b.** micrometer

  c. 1 mm = 1×10^{-3} m or 1 mm = 0.001 m
1 mm is a better representation of the length because you can use simpler numbers.

  d. 1 Mm = 1×10^6 m or 1 Mm = 1,000,000 m
2 Mm is a better representation of the length because you can use simpler numbers.

e. kilometers; 3.2 km

f. nanometers; 4.72 nm

■ Chapter 11

Math Game (Page 34)

Games vary.

Cooperative Learning (Page 35)

2. a. 1 **b.** 3; 6; 10

c. Order is not important, therefore combinations are counted. That is, if person A shakes the hand of person B, this is the same hand shake as when person B shakes hands with person A.

d. 15; 21

Research Project (Page 35)

Projects vary.

■ Chapter 12

Journal Entry (Page 36)

Turn left onto Rose Dr. At the corner, turn right onto Azalea Dr. Go through the next stop sign, turn left onto Jackson St. Travel down a steep hill, at the light, turn right onto Main St. and go north.

Cooperative Learning (Page 36)

Answers vary.

Journal Entry (Page 37)

Answers vary.

Cooperative Learning (Page 37)

3. a. $T = 3t$ **b.** $C = 16T$

c. $48t = C$ **d.** $I = 2.54$ cm

■ **Chapter 1 (Page 39)**

1. 400   **2.** 8 ft   **3.** 3   **4.** 66   **5.** 144

6. always   **7.** b and d

8. Perimeter: 20 in.   **9.** Answers vary.
Area: 28 sq in.

10. Possible answer: number cube.

■ **Chapter 2 (Page 40)**

1. $(2 + 3) \times 6 = 30$ **2.** 6   **3.** 13

4. w^7; $2^7 = 128$ **5.** $V = n^3$ **6.** >

7. Answers vary.   **8.** 14,340   **9.** $2^3 \cdot 3^2 \cdot 5$

10. sometimes

■ **Chapter 3 (Page 41)**

1. 3, 6, 9, 12, 15; 5, 10, 15, 20, 25; 15

2. always   **3.** $\frac{23}{7}$ **4.** never   **5.** $4\frac{2}{3}$

6. $\frac{13}{60}$ **7.** $\frac{1}{4}$ **8.** $4\frac{3}{4}$ **9.** $1\frac{5}{6}$ **10.** $23\frac{3}{10}$ inches

■ **Chapter 4 (Page 42)**

1. $7m - 2$ **2.** $0.30x + 20$ **3.** \$23   **4.** (3, 4)

5.

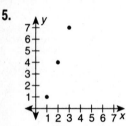

6. -1000 **7.** never   **8.** sometimes

9.

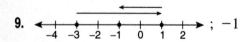

; -1

10. 4 $\boxed{+}$ 6 $\boxed{+/-}$ $\boxed{=}$; -2

■ **Chapter 5 (Page 43)**

1. about 15.9   **2.** 15.5   **3.** 16

4.

Interval	Tally	Frequency
0-9		0
10-19		0
20-29		0
30-39		0
40-49		0
50-59	I	1
60-69	II	2
70-79	TH I	6
80-89	TH II	7
90-99	IIII	4

Test Scores

5.

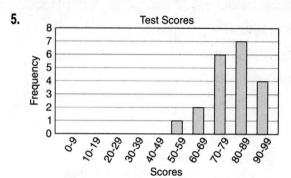

6. median

7.

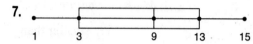

8.

(−1, 4)
(−2, −3)
(2, −2)

9. (−5, 1)

10. One or both coordinates must be 0.

■ **Chapter 6 (Page 44)**

1. $\frac{3}{4}$ **2.** $\frac{8 \text{ cm}}{11 \text{ cm}} = \frac{8}{11}$ **3.** 32 oz

4. 4 calories/gram   **5.** $x = 64$ **6.** 3 ft

7. $\frac{n}{15} = \frac{5}{3}$; $n = 25$ **8.** $x = 1.625$

9. $ry = ws$ **10.** 5 hours

■ **Chapter 7 (Page 45)**

1. $\frac{8}{25}$; 0.32   **2.** $\frac{7}{9} \approx 77.8\%$ **3.** 432

4. 29   **5.** sometimes   **6.** always

7. >   **8.** 5   **9.** 92%   **10.** 250

■ **Chapter 8 (Page 46)**

1. $\angle 1 \cong \angle 3 \cong \angle 6 \cong \angle 8 \cong \angle 9 \cong \angle 11 \cong \angle 14 \cong \angle 16$

2. sometimes   **3.** $\angle 4$

4. 3 units left and 2 units down   **5.** always

6. 12π in. ≈ 37.7 in.   **7.** $(3\pi + 6)$ in.

8. 36 sq in.   **9.** 7.25 m   **10.** some

■ **Chapter 9 (Page 47)**

1. triangles   **2.** 10   **3.** some   **4.** 104 sq in.

5. 80 sq cm   **6.** 448π sq in.

7. circumference   **8.** Cylinder B   **9.** cube

10.

Top View	Side View	Front View

■ **Chapter 10 (Page 48)**

1. always   **2.** sometimes   **3.** 2.76   **4.** <

5. −11   **6.** 7 and 3   **7.** −9   **8.** never

9.   **10.** smaller than

■ **Chapter 11 (Page 49)**

1. $\frac{1}{2}$ **2.** $\frac{2}{5}$; Experimental

3. 6

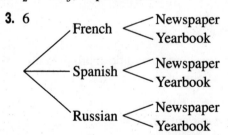

4. $\frac{1}{100}$ **5.** 24   **6.** $\frac{1}{3}$ **7.** 10! = 3,628,800

8. is not   **9.** 3   **10.** $\frac{1}{3}$

■ **Chapter 12 (Page 50)**

1. Add 6   **2.** $x = -4$

3. Multiplication by -7

4. $m = 3$ **5.** $6 + x = 10$ **6.** $x = \$4$

7. \$1.50   **8.** division   **9.** $w = 7$

10. $r = 8$ in.

Answers to Group and Individual Assessment

Chapter 1 (Page 52)

1. Answers vary. 2. 3

3. Approximately 7 granola bars.

4. Fewer. You must buy about 5 granola bars to win the poster if the letters had an equal chance of being found. In the original question it is very easy to find an E, but more difficult to find an S. Many of the bars you buy will have the letter E.

Chapter 1 (Page 53)

1. Answers vary. 2. Answers vary.

3. Answers vary. 4. 6

5. Approximately 25 packages of gum.

Chapter 2 (Page 54)

1. 0.333333 2. 3.33333 3. $3.\overline{3}$ 4. 3

5. $10y - y = 3; y = \frac{1}{3}$ 6. $\frac{1}{3}$ 7. $\frac{5}{9}$

Chapter 2 (Page 55)

1. Two digits of the number repeat.

2. Answers vary.

3. Multiply $0.\overline{23}$ by 100. Subtract $0.\overline{23}$ from the result. Divide this result by 99.

4. $\frac{23}{99}$

Chapter 3 (Page 56)

1. Answers vary.

2. The numerators and denominators are not equal to each other

3. Answers vary.

4. Yes, the cancellation method can be used if a numerator and denominator pair have any common factor.

5. Examples vary.

Chapter 3 (Page 57)

1. Answers vary. 2. Answers vary.

3. Answers vary.

4. No, when you add or subtract fractions, the numerators are eventually added or subtracted. A factor of one of the numerators is not necessarily a factor of the new numerator.

5. Counterexamples vary.

Chapter 4 (Page 58)

1. Answers vary. 2. Answers vary.

3. $a + c < b + d$; The sum of two smaller numbers is always less than the sum of two larger numbers.

4. Yes, Examples vary.

Chapter 4 (Page 59)

1. Answers vary. 2. Answers vary.

3. $a + k < b + k$; Adding the same number to both sides of an inequality does not change the original relationship.

4. Yes, Examples vary.

5. Yes, Examples vary.

Chapter 5 (Page 60)

1., 2.

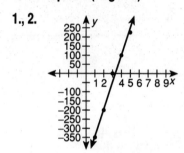

3. Answers vary, but should be approximately −450. B = your answer.

4. Answers vary, but should be approximately 150. A = your answer.

5. Answers vary.

6. Answers vary, but should be approximately a loss of $225.

Chapter 5 (Page 61)

1., 2.

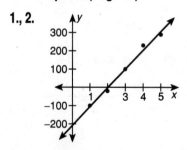

3. Answers vary. 4. Answers vary.

5. Answers vary, but should be a profit of approximately $800.

Chapter 6 (Page 62)

1.

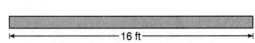

2. $\dfrac{\text{height} + \text{width}}{\text{height}} = \text{Golden Ratio}$

3. $8/h = 81/50$ or $8/h = 1.62$

4. 4.94 ft   **5.** 3.06 ft

Chapter 6 (Page 63)

1. Answers vary.

2. Plans vary.

3. In the group activity the length of material was known and both dimensions of the frame were unknown. In this problem you know the height of the frame but the width and total material length are unknown.

4. $\dfrac{3}{b} = \dfrac{81}{50}$; $b = 1.85$ **5.** 9.7 ft

Chapter 7 (Page 64)

1. 18 months

2. The 24 month option is the least expensive. It is the option with the least total repayment that also has a monthly payment under $50.

3. $1096.56, $96.56

4. $144.80, $194.72

5. $2145.60

Chapter 7 (Page 65)

1. $198.08

2. $198.08 − 96.56 = $101.52

3. It increases.

4. Statements vary.

Chapter 8 (Page 66)

1. Answers vary.

2.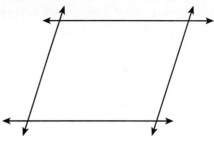

3. Answers vary.

4. Vertical angles are congruent to each other. If two parallel lines are intersected by a third line, then corresponding angles are congruent.

5. Opposite interior angles of a parallelogram are congruent.

Chapter 8 (Page 67)

1. Answers vary.

2. Answers vary.

3. Vertical angles are congruent to each other. If two parallel lines are intersected by a third line, the corresponding angles are congruent.

4. There is no relationship between the opposite interior angles of a trapezoid. The problem is that only one pair of sides is parallel. For this reason, comparisons between opposite interior angles do not follow any pattern.

Chapter 9 (Page 68)

1.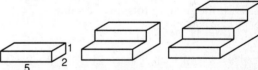

2. Volume   **3.** Answers vary.

4. Each time another step is added, add the product of 10 and the step number to the amount needed to build a staircase with one fewer steps.

5. 210 cu ft

Chapter 9 (Page 69)

1. The amount of carpeting used is a measurement of area, not volume. However, the entire surface does not need to be covered.

2. Use the area of the front and top of each step.

3. Answers vary.   **4.** Answers vary.

5. The amount of carpeting used to cover the steps is the product of 15 and the number of steps.

6. 90 square ft

■ **Chapter 10 (Page 70)**

1. The scatter plot is a V-shaped graph with its vertex at the origin.

2. The second equation sets y equal to the opposite of x's absolute value.

3. Answers vary.

4. The scatter plot is an upside down (or inverted) V with its vertex at the origin.

5. Yes, the origin is on both graphs. $|0| = 0$ and $-|0| = -0 = 0$.

6. The y-values are all negative or zero. Since $|x|$ must be positive or zero, $-|x|$ must be negative or zero.

■ **Chapter 10 (Page 71)**

1. You take the absolute value of the opposite of x.

2. Answers vary.

3. The scatter plot is a V-shaped graph with its vertex at the origin.

4. It is identical.

5. The absolute value of a number is the same as the absolute value of the number's opposite. Thus the scatter plots are the same.

■ **Chapter 11 (Page 72)**

1. $n! = n \cdot (n - 1) \cdot (n - 2) \cdot \ldots \cdot 3 \cdot 2 \cdot 1$

2. 24

3. ABC, ACB, BCA, BAC, CAB, CBA, ABD, ADB, BAD, BDA, DAB, DBA, ACD, ADC, DAC, DCA, CAD, CDA, BCD, BDC, CDB, CBD, DBC, DCB; 24

4. AB, BA, AC, CA, AD, DA, BC, CB, BD, DB, CD, DC; 12
A, B, C, D; 4

5. 1; 2; 6

6. 1; 2; 6; These are the same values as in exercise 5.

7. $P_{n,r} = \dfrac{n!}{(n - r)!}$

8. AB, BA, AC, CA, BC, CB; 6;
$P_{3,2} = \dfrac{3!}{(3 - 2)!} = \dfrac{6}{1} = 6$

■ **Chapter 11 (Page 73)**

1. 24

2. ABCD; 1

3. 24; ABC, ACD, BCD, ABD; 4

4. 12; AB, AC, AD, BC, BD, CD; 6

5. 4; A, B, C, D; 4

6. 24; 6; 2; 1

7. 4!, 3!, 2!, 1!; (Number of objects being grouped)! = $r!$

8. $C_{n,r} = \dfrac{P_{n,r}}{r!}$

9. AB, AC, BC; $C_{n,r} = \dfrac{P_{n,r}}{r!} = \dfrac{3!}{2!} = \dfrac{6}{2} = 3$

■ **Chapter 12 (Page 74)**

1. The inverse function "undoes" what the original function does.

2. 3

3. a. Adds 3.   **b.** Subtracts 3.   **c.** $y = x - 3$

4. a. $y = x - 2$ **b.** $y = x + 4$
c. $y = x - \frac{1}{3}$ **d.** $y = x + 0.6$

■ **Chapter 12 (Page 75)**

1. Answers vary, but should include the idea that an inverse function undoes what the original function does.

2. Answers vary.

3. Division by 2.

4. $y = \dfrac{x}{2}$

5. a. $y = \dfrac{x}{8}$ **b.** $y = 3x$
c. $y = \dfrac{x}{0.4}$ **d.** $y = 2.1x$